Childho
Human

D0234966

DAY LOAN

Childhood and Human Value

Development, Separation and Separability

Nick Lee

Open University Press

Open University Press
McGraw-Hill Education
McGraw-Hill House
Shoppenhangers Road
Maidenhead
Berkshire
England
SL6 2QL

email: enquiries@openup.co.uk
world wide web: www.openup.co.uk

and Two Penn Plaza, New York, NY 10121–2289, USA

First published 2005

A catalogue record of this book is available from the British Library

ISBN–13:   978 0335 21423 5 (pb)   978 0335 21424 2 (hb)
ISBN-10:   0 335 21423 1 (pb)   0 335 21424 X (hb)

Library of Congress Cataloguing-in-Publication Data
CIP data applied for

Typeset by YHT Ltd, London
Printed in Poland by OZGraf S.A.
www. polskabook.pl

Contents

Preface

The central themes of the present book became clear to me as I was finishing *Childhood and Society* (Lee 2001). In that book I had tried to develop a sociological vocabulary that would recognize the core slogan of contemporary childhood sociology – children are 'people too' – while also recognizing that the phrase 'growing up' has real referents. This made me turn my attention to the stock of ideas about development represented in the present book. The authors I have chosen seem to share an ability to think clearly about growth and change without needing to posit a hidden plan of development that awaits discovery. They also seem to share an intuition that the state of adulthood involves just as much improvisation as the state of childhood. I think 'separability' does something to unpack and to elaborate on this valuable intuition.

In the past few years two other issues occurred to me that also guided the present book. First, along with its entirely legitimate political desire to recognize children as 'people in their own right', childhood sociology also contains a reactionary impulse. It is clearly important to question familialist ideology, but this should not lead to the default assumption that all children must be in need of defence against the adults in their lives. Though, as I argue later, 'love' is no simple benevolent force, childhood sociology needs to recognize it alongside power and authority as a feature of relationships between adults and children. 'Separability' marks this concern of mine. Second, there are plenty of critical voices regarding the concept of rights. Talk about rights can cover up and reinforce inequality. It can involve garbling the message of human diversity. Likewise, it is clear that the idea of children's rights has emerged from specific cultural locations, has its limitations, does not serve every child equally and is at present little more than a promise and a hope. I take the view, however, that it is at least something to work with and to make of what we can. 'Separability' is the spin I want to put on it.

Acknowledgements

Many thanks to Laura Dent, Mark Barratt and the team at McGraw-Hill for making the production of this book such an agreeable process.

I would also like to thank Eliza and Saskia Campbell for being lovable and worth listening to.

Introduction

In 1989 the United Nations Convention on the Rights of the Child (General Assembly of the UN 1989) made it possible for children of the future to play a much more significant role in personal and in public decision-making than the children of the past had. Given the flexibility of the Convention's terms, this role can vary from such matters as having more say in which parent they live with following a divorce, all the way to significantly lowering the age of democratic majority. Yet children's rights to participate in decision-making remain controversial. Many adults think it is only right and proper that they should make decisions on behalf of children. Often, the authority that adults assume over children is understood as entirely 'natural' and is woven in with complex structures of thought and feeling, including ideas about what children are like, and convictions about appropriate relationships of respect and love.

This book focuses on the tensions regarding children's rights in what I have called the 'Western industrialized' world. The peculiar circumstances that interest me have emerged over centuries in the conjunction of democracy and capitalism. In the Western world, common sense has it that children are insufficiently 'developed' to make decisions for themselves. Consequently, the idea of children's rights is still marginal. The aim of this book is, first, to explore the roots of common-sense structures of thought and feeling about adults and children and, second, to answer this common sense with better sense derived from the work of a number of twentieth-century students of development.

Just as the contemporary common sense that would minimize children's participation in decision-making is rooted in nineteenth- and early twentieth-century understandings of development, so my hope is that, 50 years hence, common sense that would maximize children's participation in decision-making will be widely held. The following celebration and consolidation of my chosen authors are a small contribution towards this.

PART 1
POSSESSION AND SEPARATION
RESISTANCE TO CHILDREN'S RIGHTS

In Part 1, I argue that, until recently, the cultural value that children have been granted by many societies, the degree to which they have been taken to matter as people, has been closely linked to the sense that they are 'owned' by their parents, by their communities or by a state. In many instances such arrangements have granted children great value as people to love, to nurture and to care for. This has, however, also placed children in a relatively weak position wherever their economic, legal and political rights have been shaped by a culture that values them only at second hand. Rarely have their entitlements been simply their own, but instead have been contingent on their relationship with fully-fledged cultural members – adults. In the minority world of the affluent West, no less than in the majority world, the human potential of children without 'owners' is squandered for lack of financial, educational, medical and emotional investment. Having made this case, I then draw attention to the idea of 'children's rights' as formulated in the United Nations Convention on the Rights of the Child (General Assembly of the UN 1989) (hereafter, the Convention). In contrast to more familiar and time-honoured ways of valuing children, 'children's rights' tend to allow children a degree of self-possession. To be informed by children's rights is to recognize that children might, as individuals, have unique points of view and interests that are worth pursuing, regardless of adult agendas. Seen against a backdrop of more traditional ways of valuing children, 'rights' often appear to be a challenge to tradition. In the course of the late twentieth century, the apparent opposition between self-possession and possession has given rise to tension around and deep-seated resistance to the idea of children's rights. In Part 1, I attempt to describe and to account for tensions around and resistances to children's rights. I do this first because the aim of this book is to collect strategies for thinking about childhood and development that have the potential to release these tensions and to disarm this resistance.

There are limits to the forms of resistance to children's rights that I can address here. There may be opponents of children's rights who also oppose all liberal notions of human value, such as 'rights', as nothing more than the herald of Western imperialism. There may be further opponents of children's rights who see their interests as diametrically opposed to any form of individual self-determination. It is unlikely that I can influence these views. But there are many who think of themselves as friends of freedom and as children's protectors and well wishers who also view children's rights with scepticism, distaste and scorn. The arguments I present for them focus on the theme of separation. In Chapter 1, I suggest that opposition to the idea of children's rights can arise through adults' separation anxieties. For some, children's rights are to be resisted because the only alternative to the possession of children is the destruction of the bonds between parent and child. On this view, children's rights will always corrode relationships between adults and children. Clearly, if children's rights really are about separating children from adults, this view may be correct. I would argue, however, that children's rights are about establishing partial and temporary separability between children and adults rather than actual and complete separation and, thus, that these separation anxieties are not well founded.

In Chapter 2, I enquire more deeply into the reasons why we often find it difficult to tell the difference between separation and separability. Why is the idea of a person having partial and temporary separability from others not taken to be obvious or self-evident? Why is separation taken for granted while separability needs academic explication? Why, in short, does the idea of children's rights generate resistance? To answer these questions, I chart historical connections between the value placed on individuals and the degree to which they are understood as separate from and independent of others. I argue that a high value has been placed on those able to appear 'separate' across the Western world since, at least, the late nineteenth century. In consequence, those of us in pursuit of social status, those of us seeking self-determination, find it necessary to interpret our lives in terms of separation. This leads us, I will argue, systematically to mistake changes in the distribution of separability within our own lives for simple increases or decreases of separateness. When this framework of evaluation is applied to the case of children's rights, separability, and thus the compatibility of possessing children and children's self-possession are edited out, leaving nothing but grounds for anxiety.

Taken as a whole, Part 1 argues that thinking children's value through 'separability' would allow us to value children as individuals without the fear of placing all emotional and practical bonds between generations in peril. Though I am optimistic that possession and self-possession, or love and rights, can co-exist harmoniously in the pages of this book, Part 1 also exposes the historical depth and emotional strength of the commitments that can work to prevent this co-existence more generally. So this part also begins to sketch out what would need to be taken for granted about human value if in, say, 50 years, children's rights are to enjoy the broad acceptance that human rights have gained over the past 50 years. The rest of the book will fill out that outline.

1   Value and Possession

In this chapter I introduce the core issue of the book, the question of how children and childhood should be 'valued' today and in the near future. I argue that contemporary personal, cultural and institutional experience of children and childhood is informed by what appears to be a conflict between loving and caring for children and valuing children as equals, between possessing them and seeing them as self-possessed. Much that connects children to the adults who love them, many of the ways that children belong to adults, seems to be under threat from a way of valuing children that insists on recognizing them as individuals with their own opinions, demands and wishes. In this chapter, then, I describe how being loved and being, in a political sense, a minority became so closely intertwined in the case of children. We shall also see why the conflict between love and equality, a conflict that takes place in the practical realities of children's lives as much as in adults' hearts, matters so much today when social, economic and regulatory changes are reshaping relationships between generations across the globe. This should put me in a good position to reflect on the degree to which our cultures, institutions and we ourselves as individuals are 'in conflict' over children and childhood. It should also lend a little detachment that will allow me to respond creatively to contemporary controversies over children's value rather than reacting within the narrow terms of those controversies. First of all, though, I need to examine some examples of the different ways that children and childhood may be valued.

Ways of valuing children

In this section I illustrate the variety that exists in what it means to 'value' children. I describe four different ways in which children are valued: as innocents; as parental investments; as bearers of cultural and familial heritage; and, as sites of state investment. I begin by examining the connections between 'innocence' and love.

The value of innocence

> When little children are caught in a trap, when they say something foolish, drawing a correct inference from an irrelevant principle which has been given to them, people burst out laughing, rejoice at having tricked them, or kiss and caress them as if they had worked out the correct answer.
>
> (Fleury, cited in Ariès 1962: 131)

The seventeenth-century author of the above quotation was writing in stern disapproval of this treatment of children, which Ariès (1962) refers to as 'coddling'. Nevertheless, Fleury gives us a recognizable depiction of circumstances in which children might appear 'cute' or 'sweet' or 'lovably amusing'. When a child speaks in full confidence, unaware that she is making some fundamental mistake, she may amuse adults, and though she may be confused by their amusement and not feel part of it, those adults will feel able to reassure her that they are not laughing at her. Thus, in interactions where a child seems 'cute', circumstances are such that she is giving an unwitting display of her 'innocence'. This innocence may take the form of apparent cognitive incompetence, or that of insensitivity to unspoken assumptions of social interaction. Such episodes can be deeply reassuring for adults. They allow adults (and older children) to see 'innocence' in a child and 'experience' in themselves. The felt gulf between innocence and experience can only be bridged with feelings and expressions of love and reassurance. One way that children can be valued, then, is as people whose innocence draws spontaneous love and reassurance from those more experienced than them. This way of valuing children is a celebration of innocence.

I have already noted that this way of valuing children can be deeply reassuring for adults. Reassurance can be very seductive. Arguably, the Disney film versions of fairy tales have traded on this reassuring identification of childhood with innocence. Thus, some commentators have accused the Disney Corporation of a 'commodification' of childhood (Giroux 1999) in which profits are made as much by manipulating adult sensibilities and fantasies about childhood as by entertaining children. Though it would seem strange to demand that adults stop loving children and childhood because of their 'innocence', there are good reasons to question adults who reassure themselves too much. Miller (1998), for example, argues that adults' need for reassurance about childhood innocence and, indeed, about the positive moral character of the adult world, has created a special commandment for children: Thou shalt not be aware. Not only is much insight into sexuality, personal relationships and power withheld from children as a matter both of public policy and parental preference, but, further, those children who have been made 'aware' may find it very difficult to get help in understanding their experiences.

A parent's investment

Compared to other European countries, the UK has a high rate of young motherhood. Many of these younger mothers are also single parents. The consequences of having a child as a teenager are not wholly positive. Alongside the issues that face the majority of parents, such as the costs in money and time that child-rearing incurs, young mothers in the UK face extra challenges. Being a mother can reduce young women's educational attainment and thus restrict their ability to qualify for secure, lucrative employment (Cheesebrough 2003). Early child bearing also increases a woman's likelihood to be reliant on social security benefits and to live in poor housing (Cheesebrough 2003). Assuming that these young mothers have exercised some degree of choice in becoming pregnant and in carrying their pregnancy to term, we might wonder why they embark on such a costly enterprise.

Prout and Prendergast (1980) investigated just this question. They found that for the young women they spoke to, reasons for and against becoming mothers were not restricted to questions of income, education and employment. Becoming a mother was, in their eyes and in the eyes of other women in their community, a transition in identity and in status. Just as earning a wage or gaining educational qualifications are identity markers in official culture, so becoming a mother meant becoming 'somebody', having a role, being recognized and taken seriously. We might hope for social arrangements that better support young mothers or that broaden their range of identity choices. Nevertheless, this research shows that children can be valued as an investment made by parents in their own identity. There are reasons to think that this way of valuing children is broadly understood and put to use, at least in the UK, where becoming a father, or being a 'family man', connotes personal stability, reliability and trustworthiness.

So far, I have suggested that children can be valued because of what they do for their parents' identities in the present. But children can also be valued as a security against their parents' futures. The fact of ageing has long provided a rationale for having children. According to Angel and Angel (1997), before the nineteenth century in many European countries, parents would enter into formal retirement contracts with their children, passing their estates on before their death and, at the same time, specifying their children's obligations to look after them. During the twentieth century welfare systems were developed throughout the Western industrialized world to formalize and rationalize the social support of the elderly. It may have appeared that the state had taken on caring responsibilities that traditionally belonged to the children of the elderly. Currently, however, women's increased participation in the labour force and anxieties about the increasing proportion of older people in the populations of Western industrialized nations are making it clear just how much parents are still reliant on their children for both emotional and practical support.

Children and heritage

> In March 1999, Lal Jamilla Mandokhel, a sixteen-year old Pakistani girl, was repeatedly raped. Her uncle filed a complaint with the police. Police officers detained her attacker but handed Lal Jamilla over to her tribe. The council of elders decided that Lal Jamilla had brought shame on the tribe, and that the only way to overcome the shame was to put her to death. She was shot dead on the orders of the council.
>
> (Freeman 2002: 1)

This terrible episode tells us a lot about the way Lal Jamilla was valued. One aspect of her value was deemed even more important than her life. The 'council of elders' were prone to confusing guilt and innocence in cases of sexual assault. This confusion is to be found in many judicial cultures. What is more startling, perhaps, is the sense that Lal Jamilla's culpability or lack of culpability for the assault was irrelevant. Her mere involvement in a sexualized episode, unwilling though she was, was understood to have brought shame on those associated with her. Her elders clearly felt this shame themselves. Lal Jamilla was killed because she was very highly valued, not for her own sake, but as an element in an ongoing effort to assert and maintain a certain 'moral' quality across generations and over time. Arguably, she was killed because she was seen to have failed to carry her tribe's moral heritage correctly.

We may be appalled by 'honour killings' like that above, but they are extreme examples of a very widespread phenomenon. Adults can value children as inheritors of certain qualities. Sometimes the quality is an aspect of character shared by members of the same family. There might be a very strong idea of what 'we' in a family are 'like'. Sometimes the quality is a visible cultural identity. Thus, first- and second-generation immigrants may argue about standards of behaviour and clothing styles. Such is the value of cultural inheritance that its prevention has long been used as a means to subjugate colonized peoples. The Convention contains a section designed to prevent this form of subjugation. Article 30 provides that children should not be prevented from learning and participating in their parents' and grandparents' cultural traditions or from speaking their parents' language.

Children as state investments

If children are valued as the future of a culture or of a family, they are often also valued as the future population of a state. This form of valuation has given powerful adults a strong incentive to intervene in children's lives at least since the eighteenth century (Donzelot 1979). In late nineteenth- and early twentieth-century Europe, influential individuals and movements devised schemes that would variously prevent the conception of children in certain groups (Carlson 2001), select who was allowed to have children through selective sterilization (Carlson 2001), and campaign in favour of birth control for working-class women (Peel 1997). What united these schemes was a concern for the quality of a nation's future population, a desire to breed (often bogus) characteristics and types of people from the population in order to secure the future 'success' of the nation. This concern and the schemes it spawned are often called 'eugenics'.

Though eugenics is now widely understood to be both undesirable and pseudo-scientific (Carlson 2001), the active interventionist concern for the future of a state's populations that gave it justification is still with us. One of its principal areas of influence is the education system. As Jones (2003) argues, education policy in the UK, including basic decisions about the legitimate purpose of educating children, has often been shaped by policy-makers' perceptions of the economic demands that the UK would face in the short- and medium-term future. It has recently seemed appropriate to policy-makers to increase the number of formal tests children take at school, and to tie the school curriculum ever closer to the delivery of success in those tests. This has been understood to be beneficial to children, because it prepares them for the demands of the workplace, as beneficial to the education system as a whole, because it highlights poor teachers and badly-run schools, and as beneficial to the UK's future economic performance. Without wanting to tarnish UK education policy by association with eugenics, we can still observe that valuing children as a state investment continues to give policy-makers powerful justifications for shaping children's lives.

Comparing values

So far, I have examined four different ways of valuing children. The list is not intended to be exhaustive, but we can still learn something useful from it. In each case the fact that value was attached to children was no guarantee of entirely beneficial results for them. This was most clearly the case for Lal Jamilla, and perhaps for those children who, because of sexual abuse and exploitation, are no longer understood as 'innocent'. This is not to deny that children can gain from being valued as cultural inheritors, but to point out that this very much depends on the precise nature of the heritage. I would not suggest that there is something inevitably corrupt in the reassurance adults can gain from children's 'innocence'. However, it is clear that many of the ways children are valued can both give to them and take away from them as individuals. The double-edged nature of valuing children became particularly clear in the cases of parental and state investment. The parents described may have seemed selfish, but, at the same time, a parent's need to be a parent can ensure their interest in their child's well-being and make their relationship a meaningful and lasting one. Likewise, policy-makers who intervene in children's lives may seem manipulative, but when states are unable to or can see no compelling reason to play a part in shaping children's lives, the results can be appalling (Kligman 1998).

There is something else significant about these four different ways of valuing children. In each case, the value given to a child is just one feature of a broader relationship between the child and other people and institutions. I have suggested that children are valued because what they do and how they live often tell adults about themselves and about each other. An unwashed child might raise concerns about a parent because they belong to that parent. A child deemed 'immoral' might shame a whole family because they belong to that family. For good or ill, then, the ways of valuing children that I have examined so far are all about connectedness. Further, because these connections tell adults about themselves and about each other, a simple connection can in practice be lived as a relationship of possession. Parental love is, in part, made of possession. A state's care for and investment in its young are built on its possession of a population. Lal Jamilla died as a possession.

Love and rights

I have argued for two key ideas. First, that the way children are valued is part of broader sets of relationships and connections. Second, that these broader sets of relationships and connections often involve the possession of children by adults, by cultures or by institutions. I have suggested that although the possession of children can lead to appalling events, it is also an important feature of parental love and other motivations to care for children. Now that I have described the mutual implications of valuing children and possessing them, I can begin to outline the apparent conflict between loving and caring for children and valuing them as equals that I mentioned in the introduction. A brief examination of a relevant text should help us here.

Rights and separation

Laura Purdy is a political philosopher who wrote a book entitled *In their Best Interest? The Case against Equal Rights for Children* (Purdy 1992). Purdy sees herself as defending a position that has, in her view, been losing an argument over the past few decades. The argument Purdy is concerned with is between those who want to 'liberate' (1992: 8) children from adult power by providing them with 'equal rights' and those who want to 'protect' (1992: 8) children by recognizing their intrinsic needs and inabilities to wield power on their own behalf. As Purdy sees things, the liberationists are winning. She begins her book by describing an imaginary situation, or vignette, in which a 14-year-old girl, Julie, wants to leave school but her parents want her to stay in school.

> She has been studying ballet for seven years and her progress in the next two years will determine whether she is good enough to dance professionally, something her heart is set on. She considers schooling irrelevant to her future and would rather concentrate fully on her dancing. Her parents realize that staying in school does reduce her chances of success as a dancer. But they also know that most young women – even those as dedicated as Julie – drop out of ballet before they are twenty; they also know that most dance careers are short and unremunerative, so that continued schooling is in any case necessary. Julie is convinced, however, that she will persevere and have such a long and successful career that when she does finally quit, she will be in demand as a teacher.
>
> (Purdy 1992: 1)

Having set out the vignette Purdy then introduces the question her book focuses on: 'She does not now have a right to leave school. Should she have it? A surprising array of people, not just budding fourteen-year-olds agree that she should have, along with all other adult rights, the right to decide for herself whether to go to school or not' (1992: 1). Part of the craft of making an argument is getting the reader to share your perspective from the outset, or, in other words, to begin to agree with you from the beginning. So how are we to respond to the way Purdy sets up the issues? We can certainly quibble with the vignette she has constructed. She has chosen, for example, to enter her characters' lives at a point after Julie and her parents have decided that they disagree. Who knows what sort of conversation they might have had before the point at which they all made their decisions. Further indications of Purdy's perspective can be found in the words she has chosen to describe Julie and her parents' mental processes. Where Julie 'considers', 'would rather' and 'is convinced', her parents 'realize' and 'know'. Finally, we notice that the core of the drama is, even within its own imaginary terms, entirely counterfactual. Julie might want to leave school, and her parents may be concerned about that, but in fact she has no right to do so. Given this, we might see the vignette as an illustration of the current inflexibility of educational pathways that force either/or choices on people like Julie, rather than as an illustration of tensions around children's rights. What, then, can Purdy's vignette tell us?

We can read the vignette again, this time as if it were a way for Purdy indirectly to tell us about her own concerns and anxieties. Why does she set out her vignette in the way she does? First of all, she is worried that children's rights to make such decisions may well be on their way. That explains why the vignette centres on an outcome – Julie actually leaving school – that could not happen today, even within the vignette's imaginary terms of reference. Second, she is alert to the possibility that children and their parents may want different things. Third, she seems to think that, given the choice, children would do without their parents' advice, experience and knowledge. Even though Julie cannot leave school, we enter the story at the point where it is obvious that she would, despite what her parents think. Finally, Purdy is concerned that in such circumstances, parents' good intentions toward their children would go unrecognized. Even though they 'know' and 'realize', it looks like Julie will ignore them. Does Julie realize that her parents disagree with her because they love her?

If we add the emotional resonances of the vignette to the apparent imminence of 'children's equal rights', anyone who knows how Julie's parents feel is likely to be worried. The vignette is warning us of the arrival of a new way of life in which children are valued as independent, individual decision-makers. For Purdy, this new world is on its way, but it is not a happy one. Purdy is trying to show us that valuing children as individuals with their own wishes, plans and desires runs directly counter to and conflicts with more familiar ways of valuing children, the ways of valuing children that arise within parental love and which are secured by parents' possessive feelings towards their children. The world of equal rights for children seems to be an individualistic world in which parents are not recognized and family relationships count for little. It seems that 'children's equal rights' are about to dissolve relationships between parents and their children. Lonely, loveless prospects face us if parents relinquish control over their children's lives. Without possession, what relationship could there be?

Separation and anxiety

Even though I have distanced myself from Purdy (1992) to make these points about choice and separation, none of this should be taken to suggest that Purdy is unusually anxious or that her concerns are foolish. Indeed, her book successfully establishes that some of the prophets of the new world she fears do tend to interpret most adult–child relationships as oppressive by nature and would not recognize the positive side of possessive love. Further, as I will now illustrate, we currently find ourselves in social and economic circumstances that are ripe for such concerns over the possession of children by parents, cultures and institutions to flourish.

Increasing rates of divorce and separation and the subsequent re-combination of groups and persons from different families are adding new complexities to parenting and to being a child throughout the world (Giddens 1992; Smart and Neale 1999). Central to this complexity is the relationship between the possession of children and the legitimacy of adult authority. According to Smart and Neale (1999), for example, UK step-fathers, mothers' lovers or close male friends often bar themselves, or are barred from, disciplining children. Fathers retain that legitimate authority but can be out of reach just when it might be useful. The close relationship between being able to say that children are one's own, and being able to check their behaviour, a relationship of possessive love and care, is thus put under some strain. Television also has a part to play. Affluent parents in the West and elsewhere may find that the social worlds presented to children through contemporary cable and satellite television differ markedly from their own. While children do not simply repeat what they see and are aware of differences between fiction and fact from an early age (Buckingham 2000), the screen can provide children with fresh behavioural resources to use in their interactions with parents and with each other, including patterns of speech and modes of social evaluation. Thus television may be understood as separating children from parents by offering an alternative source of authority on matters of personal conduct. On what basis, other than possession, can parents reassert their authority, should they wish to?

In the past few decades, both the rate and the nature of migration have changed. One mid-twentieth-century standard form of migration involved the largely planned and formalized movement of citizens of former colonies in the majority world to take up employment in former colonial countries of the minority world. Today, such factors as the break-up of the former Soviet Union, the destabilization of some parts of the Muslim world and the collapse of regimes built on a superpower's support during the Cold War are generating a more complex set of migratory patterns. Whatever form migration takes, it raises questions of cultural identity and belonging. Arguably, these are exacerbated as migration becomes more haphazard and dangerous. When we consider the 'development' of majority world economies, we find that with overseas investment from multinational corporations, more women are being given opportunities to take up paid employment (Castells 1996). This form of modernization often raises questions about 'traditional' patriarchal relations in which men have assumed ownership of their wives, female relatives and children (Castells 1997). Finally, in one of the largest, yet least discussed, instances of global social change, AIDS and HIV are cutting a swathe through the populations of many Sub-Saharan African countries and are a growing threat elsewhere. Whole generations of children have been and are being orphaned (Barnett and Whiteside 2002).

There are many reasons today, then, for a wide range of people in many parts of the world to be concerned about the maintenance of bonds between generations. There may be concern that parents are hampered in raising their children by such factors as popular culture or the break-up of families. This concern can generate a desire, sometimes a nostalgic desire (Smart and Neale 1999), to re-affirm adults' possession of their children. Migrant populations may quite understandably fear the loss of their cultural identity, the practices and beliefs that give them a sense of their place in the world, and might seek to emphasize to their children just how much they belong to all those who share their ethnicity or religion. Where 'modernization' means the prospect of women having paid employment outside the home, 'traditional' patri-archies may respond with political or violent means to reassert their owner-ship of their families. Where a generation of parents has been decimated by disease, we might well wonder what will happen to those children who have no obvious possessors to take responsibility for them. Thus, many current social issues involving children are liable to generate 'separation anxieties' for adults. One way for adults to defend themselves from separation anxiety is to reassert the desirability and propriety of ways of valuing children that treat them as possessions, to will 'family values' or 'tradition' back into existence. Another defence lies in being scornful or mocking about children's rights (Alderson 2000). For example, Purdy allows that some of her readers might find children's rights 'ludicrous' (1992: 2). In this context it is clear that any way of valuing children that seems to deviate from the possessive norm is likely to be disturbing. This is the shape and scale of the conflict of values that informs children's lives today.

Provision, protection and participation

So far, I have examined some of the variety that exists in ways of valuing children, I have argued that value and possession are often understood as closely linked and that, in so far as they threaten this link, current social and economic contexts are liable to provoke feelings of separation anxiety among adults. I suggested that this separation anxiety can lead to an intensification of desire to possess, and thus to protect and to control children. Recent de-velopments in the regulation of relationships between children, individual adults, cultures and institutions, however, also need consideration. As I will suggest, the 1989 United Nations Convention on the Rights of the Child (henceforth, 'the Convention') certainly affirms the picture of a child's value that might seem second nature or common sense to a parent, but it also seeks to recognize and value children as individuals who may possess preferences, wishes, plans and, above all, themselves.

Protection and provision: legitimating possession

At the time of writing, all member states of the United Nations except the USA are signatories to the Convention. This means that these states have all committed themselves to the 54 articles it contains. These commitments are often broken down into three categories: rights to protection, rights to provision and rights to participation. Examples of rights to protection can be found in Article 19, which is a promise by the signatories to work against the abuse and neglect of children, and in Article 8, which is a promise to protect children's identity so that their name, nationality and family relations cannot be taken from them. Examples of rights to provision can be found in Article 24, which details rights to health care, and Article 28, which establishes children's rights to education. Though the implementation of these rights to protection and provision may be difficult, they are not in themselves especially controversial. They are in accordance with, and reinforce a loving and caring approach to children. Further, they draw a distinction between forms of possession that may be good for children and forms of possession that involve or can lead to children's exploitation. For example, just as Article 11 combats trafficking in children, or the 'illicit transfer and non-return of children abroad', so Article 21 allows that properly supervised and controlled inter-country adoption may take place. The Convention may be seen as an attempt to regulate the value of children, specifically, to maximize the positive outcomes of the possession of children and to minimize the negative outcomes. By discriminating between good and bad forms of possession, these rights to protection and provision help to clarify and legitimate some quite familiar ways of valuing children.

Children's participation

As we might have come to expect, rights to participation often raise a more ambivalent and less sympathetic response than those to protection and provision (Goonsekere 1998; Alderson 2000). So let us examine them. Article 15 recognizes children's rights to free association and peaceful assembly. These are the rights one would require to attend a political, cultural or religious meeting or to participate in a political demonstration free from interference by state agents or by other citizens. Article 14 is a promise to respect children's freedom of thought, conscience and religion. This is a broad commitment against the criminalization and/or persecution of children for having different beliefs or perspectives than countries' ruling elites. It also preserves parents' and guardians' rights and duties to guide the child in the use of this right in a manner 'consistent with the evolving capacities' of the child. Article 13 promises children freedom of expression, so that they may declare and publicize their beliefs, perspectives and opinions without fear of persecution. In each case these rights are to be restricted only by such considerations as the rights of others, public safety and order and national security and may be restricted only by agents so empowered by the state's legal code.

Section 1 of Article 12 reads as follows: 'States Parties shall assure to the child who is capable of forming his or her own views the right to express those views freely in all matters affecting the child, the views of the child being given due weight in accordance with the age and maturity of the child.' This allows children to have a say in decisions that affect them. It allows that, in some circumstances, children might have different views and opinions than all the other people who surround them and that, when those circumstances arise, that difference should be heard in any 'judicial' or 'administrative' proceedings affecting the child, as Section 2 of Article 12 has it. This does not mean that other people's views are always irrelevant. It does not mean that children have to make all decisions on their own. It most certainly does not mean that children's opinions will always be triumphant. After all, the article requires that the weight given to children's views be moderated in line with their age and maturity. Considered in terms of the actual threat this poses to adults' possession of children, this really is a very modest proposal. Like many of the protection and provision rights described above, it is concerned not just to guard against bad exploitative forms of possession but also to legitimize good forms of adults' possessive concern for children. So why have children's participation rights been received with such ambivalence?

Separation and separability

Rights to participation seem rather different from those to protection and provision. 'Protection' conjures an image of children surrounded by adults who ward off dangers that children alone would be helpless to defend themselves from. 'Provision' has the children once again surrounded and being nourished with food, information, and so on that they might be unable to obtain for themselves. In these images, children's lack of competence forms the backdrop of protection, provision and of surrounding possessiveness. Although 'participation' does not suggest the absence of adults, it does suggest a situation in which children are *with* adults rather than surrounded by them, accompanied rather than possessed.

To begin to answer the question about the reception of children's participation rights, it is worth reviewing Article 12. I have suggested that one of its functions is to legitimate 'good' possessive relationships between adults and children. We now need to examine how it is supposed to do this. Under what circumstances might a court or administrative decision-making body need to hear the freely expressed views of a child? Wherever an adult's ignorance, vested interest or malign intent would prevent them from delivering information that would bear on a decision that affects a child's life, the child's interests would clearly require that she speak for herself. Where the adults in question are close to the child and have some possession of the child, for the child to speak for herself and not be spoken for requires a temporary alteration of that relationship. Instead of being 'surrounded' by adults as they speak, a position that could always muffle or distort their words, they may be 'with' or even 'against' that adult. Under the provisions of Article 12 the normal expectations of a possessive relationship can be suspended. One of the benefits of this suspension is that it provides a way of checking to make sure that a relationship that is normally a possessive one is of a positive rather than a negative quality and outcome for the child. Thus the temporary suspension of possession has the potential to make possession legitimate. But in order for this to occur, it is necessary to suppose that children are, in principle, separable from the adults who normally possess them. Children's self-possession, as described by the Convention, is based not on their separation as individuals from others but on their separability as individuals from others. While I have focused on situations involving adult parents, the same reasoning applies in Article 12 to relations between state employees and children.

Given what I have argued above about adult separation anxieties, it seems likely that ambivalent or even hostile reactions to children's rights or equality in general and children's participation rights in particular are, in part, reactions against the separation of children from those adults who would normally possess them. But, if the picture I have drawn of children's rights is correct, these reactions are misplaced. It would seem that children's rights to participation in making decisions that affect them can generate opposition because people find it difficult to distinguish between separability and actual and complete separation.

Conclusion

In this chapter I have discussed many issues concerning the value of children. I have been particularly concerned to identify, describe and understand an apparent conflict between loving and caring for children and valuing them as individuals. Throughout the discussion I have emphasized the fact that for many adults, building and maintaining relationships with their children is one of their most significant and enduring activities, whether they see their children predominantly as their individual possession and responsibility, or as the possession and responsibility of their culture or family. This is why I have at no point suggested that 'possessiveness' in adult–child relationships is wrong in itself. I have no interest in increasing anxieties about separation and loss that are being generated in our world today.

Nevertheless, I have spent time arguing in favour of something that can clearly be experienced as a threat to relationship, a challenge to possessive love – the conjunction of the words 'children' and 'rights'. I have addressed the topic of children's value as if there were no real need to fear for love and to defend it against equality, and I have proceeded as if it were possible to recognize both possession and self-possession without contradiction. What has emerged from my discussion, then, is a need for a 'flexible' way of seeing connections between adults and children. A 'brittle' view of connections can make one defensive, and can lead one to mistake separability for actual and complete separation. This is because a brittle connection always threatens to snap. A more flexible view would see all human connections, each separation and each attachment, as 'partial' (Strathern 1991). 'Partial separations' would be limited to particular spaces and to particular times, none would be total but they would be no less real and significant for that. On this flexible view, it is clear that, at times, separability can help reinforce attachment, just as Article 12 helps legitimate the good in adults' possession of children.

But there is more to this story than an injunction to 'be flexible'. If I want to flesh out this way of thinking and feeling about relationships between adults and children, I need to understand why we might be 'brittle' in our thinking about those connections in the first place. If it is clear that separability and separation are not the same, if it is clear that one may be in possession but not possess totally, how is it that confusion about these issues is possible? In the next chapter I will address just this question, asking why separation matters so much to us.

2　Value and Separation

Introduction

It is a commonplace of sociological (Bourdieu 1984) and anthropological (Lévi-Strauss 1986) research that human communities create value by dividing people, things and activities into categories such as 'male and female', 'raw and cooked' or 'cultured and uncultured'. Striking examples of the creation of value around the categories 'male' and 'female' can still be found in many Western societies where men and women are often seen as properly having distinctive emotional and intellectual characteristics. As many who have not been convinced of the pertinence of these categories have found to their cost, while supposedly 'masculine' characteristics in men and 'feminine' ones in women are highly valued, a 'masculine' woman or a 'feminine' man is open to scorn and persecution. Such is the significance of separation in the creation of value and in the assignment of value to persons. If one confirms the gender separation by trying to live as a 'masculine man' or 'feminine woman', few will take issue. If through one's conduct, however, one suggests that the separation in question is conventional and changeable rather than natural and inevitable, one risks being treated as 'unnatural' and monstrous.

Reflecting on what I argued in the previous chapter, it is not too hard to see just such a monster in the figure of a 'child with rights', one who crosses the divide between adult and child, breaking connections with their parents, asserting their independence in defiance of all 'natural' love and law. But, as I suggested towards the end of the chapter, if it exists at all, this monstrous child does not have its origins in written laws and regulations. As we saw, there is little in the Convention to fear and much to celebrate, as long as one bears in mind that the Convention insists on the partial and temporary separability of children, not on their actual and complete separateness or separation from others. Children's separability can help to legitimate the possessive love of those who extend a claim on them just as it rules against possessive exploitation. I closed the chapter, however, by asking what makes it difficult to register a difference between actual and complete separation and separability.

In this chapter I offer a fairly simple, if surprising, answer to this question. I argue that it is easy for many adults to mistake children's partial and temporary separability for actual and complete separation because our status and identity as adults involve acting, on occasion, as if we were no-one else's possession, as if we were reliant on no other, independent in our decisions and thus entirely responsible for ourselves. Since everyone depends on someone for something, since there is no actual and complete separation, to be an 'adult', to pass as responsible and independent, is to participate in a strategic confusion of separability and separateness. We allow each other the high value of full adult cultural membership, as long as we are able, when appropriate, to pretend that we are actually and completely separate from one another. A fixation on separation or independence as a desirable condition tends to reduce the subtlety of our thoughts and feelings about possession and separability, love and rights with significant consequences for children's cultural position.

My first move in making this case is to take a step back in time. In the previous chapter I argued that there is an apparent conflict between love and equality in today's world. I will now ask how that situation has arisen, how it is that we can know at one and the same time that children are possessions and that they have rights. To answer this we need a little history.

Where do rights come from?

According to the political theorist Charles Taylor (Taylor and Gutmann 1992), not only does the value assigned to different people vary within and between societies and over historical time, but it is also possible to detect distinct principles underlying the distribution of that value. These principles establish how people are to be categorized and/or considered separate from one another. Taylor argues that where once European societies distributed human value according to a principle of 'honour', contemporary Western societies distribute human value according to a principle of 'dignity'. In societies defined by honour, such as late medieval England or France, 'what we now call identity was largely fixed by one's social position. That is, the background that explained what people recognised as important to themselves was to a great extent determined by their place in society and whatever roles or activities attached to this position' (Taylor and Gutmann 1992: 31).

The sort of societies Taylor has in mind here are monarchies. In a monarchy, if one amounted to anything much, it was by virtue of one's birth and breeding, the proximity of one's family, by descent or association, to the monarch. Not only were life chances distributed on this basis, but so were legal positions, such as the ability to own property and to extract profit from what one owned. Honour was intrinsically linked to inequality. For the nobility to enjoy a high level of social esteem, for them to be considered persons of value, it was necessary that common people were understood as less valuable and were given lesser consideration. The degree to which a person was understood to be worth consulting and listening to in matters that would affect their lives was determined by their place in the honour system, with a noble counting far more than a commoner.

The distribution of human value according to honour had consequences for the value of children. Ariès (1962) is well known for making the controversial (see Shahar 1992) argument that there was no concept of childhood in the Middle Ages. As he built his argument, he drew on portraits of children of the French nobility, in which they appear in clothing and jewellery that is just as symbolic of honour as that worn by adult nobility in their portraits. Whatever the merits of Ariès' thesis overall, it seems that in an honour system a person's age was largely irrelevant to their value and status. For honorific purposes at court any distinction between child and adult was irrelevant, even if a very young noble was in practice rarely consulted about affairs of state. Turning to the case of the common people, if distinctions were made between adults and children, they would have very little effect on the matter of being taken seriously as a person whose opinions and feelings were worth listening to, since adult commoners scarcely enjoyed that privilege.

For Taylor, the transition from the medieval, feudal world to the modern world was marked by the collapse of honour and the emergence of dignity as a principle for the distribution of human value. Where some people had honour and some had none, dignity is taken to be both the possession of, and what is owed to, each and every person regardless of the conditions of their birth. Not only does the dignity principle hold title and nobility irrelevant to questions of human value, but it is also supposed to give equal value to each and every person regardless of gender, ethnicity, sexuality, physical ability, and so on. Though Taylor may be too optimistic about the depth to which dignity has re-ordered questions of human value in the West, the notion of the inherent dignity of human beings at least makes any system of preference that is not visibly based on merit appear illegitimate. Crucially, for our concerns, although it is clear that people may belong to and identify with the categories of age, gender, ethnicity, and so on, the notion of dignity should prevent judgements being made about people on the basis of such memberships. The observance of dignity requires us to allow that persons are separable from these categories of membership, belonging and affiliation whenever decisions are made regarding their worth. Without this separability, which in no way adds up to actual and complete separation, there would be nothing to prevent the denial of, say, political representation to a person who happened to belong to a certain ethnic group. Where Taylor's honour was based on a rigid separation between categories of person (noble and commoner) and the subsumption of each and every person to a category, dignity, as Taylor describes it, requires us to grant that there are different categories of people, such as the category 'children', but also requires us to be careful to recognize that those categories are not always relevant because individuals should not be subsumed within them. Dignity, then, requires us to distinguish between separability and separation. Further, dignity requires us to deploy separability, to be able temporarily and strategically to detach individuals from categories of person. This operation allows us to avoid having group characteristics imposed on us and to avoid imposing them on others. Children's separability, such as is advanced by the Convention, is a consequence of their recognition as humans with dignity.

How was possession preserved?

So far I have followed Taylor's work on the distribution of human value. I have suggested that egalitarian views of the value of children arose as a consequence of the replacement of honour with dignity. The ideas of 'human rights' and 'children's rights' are a recent product of a process of social modernization that has been underway for several hundred years, with varied rates and effects in different parts of the world. But I have come no closer to understanding how a view of children as possessions can co-exist with this egalitarian view. For my purposes, Taylor's account of changing principles behind the distribution of human value needs to be supplemented.

The modernization of European societies, along with the development of dignity and representative democracy, is inseparable from the history of European colonialism (Larrain 1990). For four hundred years, European states spread their trading networks through military and economic conquest. European military leaders and economic explorers, who were themselves often beneficiaries of the principle of honour, were to meet, trade with and eventually subjugate societies that operated their own versions of monarchy and the principle of honour. One feature of a system of honour, run in isolation, is that it guarantees the unquestioned superiority of the upper ranks. The problem that colonialism raised for European honour was that of how to downgrade the members of the nobility of societies that so closely resembled colonists' own in their honour-based distribution of human value. The problem was resolved with the invention of a novel principle for the distribution of human value that I call 'level of development'. This principle allowed for the attribution of high value to any human who could be seen as highly 'developed' in terms of human evolutionary history, in terms of the culture that they belonged to, or, as we shall see, in terms of their age. To mark some people as highly developed, it was necessary to mark others as less developed. Said illustrates this well;

> On the one side of the colonial divide was a white Christian Europe whose various countries . . . controlled most of the earth's surface. On the other side of the divide, there was an immense variety of territories and races, all of them considered lesser, inferior, dependent,

subject. White colonies such as Ireland and Australia too were considered made up of inferior humans; a famous Daumier drawing for instance explicitly connects Irish whites and Jamaican blacks. Each of these lesser subjects was classified and placed in a scheme of peoples guaranteed scientifically by scholars and scientists like Georges Cuvier, Charles Darwin and Robert Knox.

(1993: 162)

As a supplement to honour, a racist version of 'level of development' reached its peak in the late nineteenth century, growing from the need to legitimate conquest, to inspire underlings, and from sheer triumphalism. It allowed for the belief that Europeans' remarkable success in the business of imperial and colonial exploitation merely reflected a natural order. It gave consolation and confidence to the regular soldier or colonial functionary who, when in doubt, could always tell himself that though colonized peoples may have their own social hierarchies, the best of 'theirs' would never be a match for a regular 'Englishman'.

These developments had their impact on issues of human value within European countries too. Increased trade and processing of traded commodities were strengthening the industrialist classes in the eighteenth and nineteenth centuries, especially in the UK. Aristocratic hierarchy was being challenged by wealthy commoners. Rapid social mobility can be unsettling. It challenges existing conceptions of self-worth and the value and respect merited by others. The notion of 'level of development' was useful here in subtly reshaping the boundaries of respect. It opened a way to detect a shared quality among those who would otherwise be rigidly separated by degrees of honour, while also maintaining distinction from the domestic working class. Though all Englishmen were of high value, being bred from the same stock, some were marked by their lack of moral development, idleness, indiscipline, and so on. A scale of moral development was laid on top of a scale of cultural development, which was laid on top of scale of 'racial' development to secure the position of white, adult, middle-class male not only as superior to others but, vitally, as notionally equal to one another in their ability to govern and direct themselves. As a principle for the distribution of human value, level of development could accommodate noble, soldier and industrialist alike, easing their cooperation, exchange of favours and shared command of the state. The 'equals' shared a quality variously conceived of as moral, intellectual and racial, a quality of self-governance and initiative, of independence from the claims, wishes and commands of others. The highest level of development in English imperialism was represented by a man capable of making and proving himself – a gentleman.

The gentleman was a transitional figure between principles of honour and of dignity. He was at once capable of claiming honour and position among nobility without relying entirely for that honour on the circumstances of his birth, and full of a dignity won by his works, respected by his notional equals. Level of development helped to smooth over the contradictions between the principles of honour and dignity. With the useful and timely fiction of the independent individual gentlemen in place, any who found themselves in the position of depending on another for income or of having to follow another's instructions would not have to look far to find a ready explanation for their position. In that they differed from the independent gentleman, they were less developed than him on either an evolutionary or lifecourse timescale, and were thus constitutionally unable to make decisions about the shape of their own lives. It was right and proper that such dependents cultivate the meek and obedient habits of human possessions, desirous of the love and fearful of the wrath of the father.

It appears then that the nineteenth century saw a revival of the patriarch as the owner of self and of others that previous societies (Miller 1999) had incorporated, boosted this time by emerging sciences of human nature and their concern to distinguish 'primitive' people and societies from 'developed' people and societies. In the UK at least, the 'level of development', with its acme in the figure of the gentleman, preserved patriarchy long into the process of modernization and created a block on the application of universalist conceptions of human dignity to the cases of women and children. That contemporary children are seen *both* as possessions *and* as bearers of rights is a consequence of Taylor's main current of modernization that leads from the principle of honour to the principle of dignity meeting the complex conservative identity strategies developed by the powerful in response to that main current.

Development and the human sciences

Now that I have described three principles of human value and placed them in an historical context, it should be clear just how important it was for one type of high status nineteenth-century adult to assert his independence and separateness. I have not indicated, however, quite how this identification of separateness with high status gained credibility beyond the immediate circumstances of its production. Why, with European empires all but vanished, does 'level of development' still have resonance? One way to address this issue is to examine some examples of nineteenth- and early twentieth-century sciences of human nature where questions of development were explicitly raised. So in the next two sections I shall examine Freud (1962) and Piaget (1927), two writers often described as founders of developmental psychology.

Freud and the primal horde

> There are men still living who, as we believe, stand very near to primitive man, far nearer than we do, and whom we therefore regard as his direct heirs and representatives. Such is our view of those whom we describe as savages or half-savages; and their mental life must have a peculiar interest for us if we are right in seeing in it a well-preserved picture of an early stage of our own development.
>
> (Freud 1962: 1)

While Freud was no racist, he certainly was concerned with 'level of development'. The lines above, for example, provide a neat illustration of the way that 'level of development' helped Europeans to identify some of their contemporaries who lived differently from them (savages and half-savages) with the deep past of human evolutionary development. Freud chose to begin his investigation into the origin of 'taboos' by examining the definitions of and prohibitions against incest among 'the most backward and miserable of savages, the aborigines of Australia, the youngest continent, in whose fauna too we can still observe much that is archaic and that has perished elsewhere' (Freud 1962: 1). As well as leading us to wonder how well Freud would have fared if asked to find food, drink and shelter and navigate hundreds of miles of apparently featureless Australian scrub while avoiding archaic fauna, this second quotation also establishes an intimate connection between very old things and very young things, a connection that might at first seem odd. For Freud, very old things that have been preserved and very young things have one thing in common; neither of them have done much developing, and so both can be considered 'primitive'. Freud relies implicitly upon this connection as he builds his argument, drawing in infants and children as he goes. It is occasionally made explicit, as when he describes 'the horror of incest' displayed by 'savages' as 'essentially an infantile feature' (Freud 1962: 17).

I have chosen to examine *Totem and Taboo* because it is here that Freud develops an account of the origin of 'right' or 'law' (Freud 1962: 38), an account, which as we shall see, also narrates the development of men (*sic*) from an original 'primitive' stage, to a stage in which they are both psychologically independent, in the sense of being able to control their own impulses, and equal before the law. Over the course of the first few chapters, Freud establishes that in many 'savage' societies there exist activities, persons and things that are 'taboo'. The distinguishing feature of a 'taboo' is that the person who believes in it, believes that if they break the taboo by performing an action or by touching a person or a thing that is deemed taboo, then punishment, perhaps death, will follow automatically, whether or not fellow believers deliberately carry out that punishment. Taboo breakers will receive punishment and the spirit world or plain luck will administer it whatever fellow believers do. This belief presents a strong incentive to observe taboos and to watch oneself carefully so that one does not break them accidentally. One of the most common taboos concerns incest, which is variously defined by different cultures as inappropriate contact with, sight of or sexual intercourse with a relative, who may be a blood relative, and/or a fellow member of some other recognized grouping or 'totem'. But what accounts for this horror of incest? What accounts for the power of taboo?

Freud's explanation begins with Charles Darwin's views on the social structure adopted by primitive humans. Darwin (1871) suggested that in the distant past, humans, or their near ancestors, lived much as gorillas do today, in small groups or 'hordes' in which one male alone has sexual relations with all the females. The dominant male defends his exclusive sexual rights in periodic single combat with younger males. The younger males are presented with an alternative; either to leave their horde in search of a weaker opponent; or, to remain and wait until the dominant male weakens, testing his strength as often as they are able. In Freud's terms this social structure was the 'primal horde' in which 'a violent and jealous father ... keeps all the females for himself and drives away his sons as they grow up' (1962: 141). There is no direct evidence of the existence of a primal horde among humans or their near ancestors, but for Freud there is plenty of evidence today of primitive humans living in tribes consisting of bands of males in which each male has the same rights and the same duty to respect taboos as every other. Freud reasons that the primal horde gave way to this second, 'tribal' social structure through many violent revolutions of the following kind: 'One day the brothers who had been driven out came together, killed and devoured their father and so made an end of the patriarchal horde. United, they had the courage to do and succeeded in doing what would have been impossible for them individually' (Freud 1962: 141). The brothers now had access to women. But what was to prevent the brothers from fighting among themselves and repeating the cycle? It is at this point that Freud relies on the connection he sees between the very old and the very young and, incidentally, the 'neurotic'. By talking to his psychoanalytic patients, Freud found that children and 'neurotics' alike have ambivalent feelings toward their fathers. They both love and hate their fathers. He then supposes that those primal brothers had the same ambivalence toward the dominant male, who has by now been unambiguously identified by Freud as their father. They hated their father for having power over them and for denying them women, but they also loved and admired him. Once they had killed him and satisfied their hatred, their love took over and filled them with remorse. Their guilt led them to create two taboos. The first was a taboo against harming a 'totem' animal identified as the symbol of the dead father. The second was the incest taboo. This allowed them to repent of the murder by doing what the dead father would command of them were he still alive – keeping away from his women.

Though much of Freud's story takes place in the distant past, it ends up endorsing certain associations of equality, independence and order that are still made today. The violent hierarchical conditions of the primal horde were superseded by a peace that was guaranteed by men's ability independently and as individuals to control themselves, their desires and their behaviour. Freud's 'development' then was brought about by the interactions of men and ended by bringing men into a state of equal value and responsibility for themselves.

At this point I should register some scepticism about Freud's account of the origin and strength of taboo. We need to recognize first that, effectively, Freud has added two untested hypotheses of his own to Darwin's and that, although this cluster of hypotheses makes sense of the phenomenon of taboo, there are many evidential holes in the fabric of argument. Indeed, Freud is often criticized as being unscientific (Eysenck 1985) and accused of being underhanded in making claims that, for want of evidence, simply cannot be shown to be false (Popper 1963). Second, taken as a whole, *Totem and Taboo* relies on an identification between primal social processes and the thinking and feelings of children and 'neurotics', an assumption, in other words, that there is a category of 'primitives' who all share the same basic attributes. We may not feel this assumption is justified. Finally, we should note that where feminist writers often point out that women have been written out of history, it takes Freud to write them out of prehistory too. On Freud's account, women simply have no active part to play in changing social structure. It is interesting that Freud briefly considers an alternative hypothesis that does see women as active (1962: 142) but rejects Atkinson's (1903) suggestion that the tension between the paternal tyrant and his sons was eased by a mother encouraging the tyrant to tolerate the presence of other males.

It is not my main aim here to judge Freud, however, but to learn how his work won credibility for the idea of 'level of development' and strengthened the association between separation and high status. Consider how taboo arose. A number of young men gathered together to kill their father. Once they had killed him, they dealt with their guilt by inventing taboo. The taboo, law or code was of such a form that each man controlled his own actions because he was frightened of an immediate and automatic punishment. There was no need for these men to threaten or control each other, because each controlled himself. Rather than accept the threat of violence from their father, these sons had created an impersonal code within which each and every one of them was equally subject to a control that each exerted over himself. So just as Freud narrates the origins of law and of civilization, he also narrates the origins of the psychologically independent individual. The lesson is that whatever community or brotherhood takes place in civilized societies, it takes place on the basis of the basic separateness of men. Powerful nineteenth-century European men might well have rejected this murky and frightening myth as a true account of the origin of civilization. After all, it risks portraying empire and colonialism not as Christian civilizing missions, but as a tribal alliance of 'brothers' in violence against the rest of the world. Nevertheless, Freud has given us an origin myth of independent individuals united in their respect for the law and in their responsibility for themselves. Individual separation, civilization and a high level of development go hand in hand in this myth. In Freud's hands, the association between them becomes, temporarily at least, an article of respected science.

Piaget, chaos and discrimination

> The transition from chaos to cosmos ... is brought about through an elimination of egocentrism.
>
> (Piaget 1927: xiii)

Just as Freud had no direct access to the pre-historical origins of civilization, so Piaget had no direct access to the experiences of a new-born child. His enviably influential research programme, however, was built on a bold hypothesis about the minds and experiences of new-born children. Consider the following quotation:

> Let us imagine a being, knowing nothing of the distinction between mind and body. Such a being would be aware of his desires and feelings but his notions of self would undoubtedly be much less clear than ours. Compared with us he would experience much less the sensation of the thinking being within him, the feeling of a being independent of the external world. The knowledge that we are thinking about things severs us in fact from the actual things.
>
> (Piaget 1927: 37)

The being Piaget imagines for us is a baby. Piaget hypothesized that when babies are born, they are not yet able to tell the difference between themselves and the rest of the world. Piaget calls this lack of discrimination 'egocentrism'. In Piaget's terms, babies are 'egocentric' but not because they think they are the most important person in the world. Rather, they are 'egocentric' because they are not aware of a difference between themselves and the rest of the world. For Piaget, then, the process of individual development is one in which children create a distinction between themselves and the rest of the world and elaborate on it as their experience grows. Subsequent development is made up of many different transitions which share the same basic form; from experiencing the world as an undifferentiated chaos to experiencing the world as having an implicate order. For Piaget, these transitions are made possible by an initial discovery of one's separation from the rest of the world.

As with Freud, my purpose in examining Piaget's work is not to criticize him as a scientist (see Gopnick and Meltzoff, 1998, for more recent assessments of his work). Rather, my interest is in what Piaget did with the theme of separation and its association with human value. In my account so far I have suggested that Freud (1962) was concerned with changes in social structure and the moral and emotional consequences of the emergence of responsible individuals, separate and equal before the law. I will now suggest that Piaget was principally concerned with the emergence of a form of thought called 'reason' which is to be distinguished from other forms of thought such as 'magic' and 'animism'. For Piaget, reason is founded on the comprehension that self and world are different and are thus properly differentiated from one another. Other forms of thought lack a comprehension of that difference.

Once he has presented us with his imaginary baby-being, Piaget goes on to list some of the consequences of its egocentric inability to distinguish itself from the rest of the world:

> [T]he psychological perceptions of such a being would be entirely different from our own ... words would be bound up with things and to speak would mean to act directly on these things. Inversely, external things would be less material and would be endowed with intentions and will.
>
> (1927: 37)

Piaget gives a list of the kinds of 'magical' thought that he found children using. Some children were under the impression that they could affect events in the world merely by thinking. Others performed certain actions or said certain words in attempts to influence events that they desired or feared. In each case there is no 'intelligible causal relation' (1927: 132) at work, rather, the children's magical thought relies on a sense of 'participation' or connection between their minds and actions and events in the rest of the world. The other consequence of a failure to distinguish oneself from the world is the belief that inanimate objects possess senses, will or consciousness of their own. Piaget discusses this under the heading 'animism'. He lists four stages of development that children go through as they build their sense of distinction and discard magical participative thought. At first everything is deemed conscious, then only moving things are so understood. Third, a distinction is drawn between things that move of their own accord, like the sun and wind and are granted consciousness while those that, like wheelbarrows, need a shove, are denied it. In the final stage, consciousness is restricted to the animal world.

So far I have shown that, like Freud, Piaget gave 'separation' a good deal of explanatory power. But to what extent do his developmental ideas make more general decisions about human value? Does he, like Freud, gather different kinds of 'primitives' together? Piaget adopted the terms 'magic', 'participation' and 'animism' from the anthropologist Lévy-Bruhl who helped refine them as technical terms for the study of 'primitive peoples' (Piaget 1927: 169). However, Piaget did not collapse child development onto human evolution or cultural development, despite his adoption of anthropological terms. He insists that there is a difference between the child's thought and 'primitive' thought and that, though others may confound them, he does not. To the extent that he is able to hold back such easy associations here, Piaget is consistent with his general tendency to control the place of questions of human value in his research. He studies children not to show that they are less than adults, but to show that they are different. In a similar manner he is concerned to preserve a possible difference between children and 'primitives' even as he adopts anthropological terms. It is clear, however, that for Piaget, tendencies to magical, animistic and participative thought in general must be controlled if we are to have access to reason, a way of thinking that is both self-consistent and consistent with the facts of the world. Though Piaget clearly values children's difference from adults, he also values one form of thought above others. Reason is the end point of individual cognitive development and can only be made and preserved through a decisive split between one's understanding of oneself and one's understanding of the world.

Human value and separation: a summary

Now that I have examined some of Freud and Piaget's work I can summarize my argument so far. I have argued that as the idea of shared human dignity spread, replacing the rigid hierarchies of honour, so its tendency to equalize human value was countered by the growth of 'level of development'. 'Level of development' gained credibility because it offered answers to two questions of vital importance to powerful Europeans of the nineteenth and early twentieth centuries. The questions of the origins of civilization and of the origins of reason were vital questions for societies that drew their wealth from those they considered uncivilized and unreasoning. Freud provided an account of the origins of civilization and the rule of law and Piaget provided an account of the origins of reason. Both accounts were founded on the possibility of individuals being 'separate' from one another and psychologically independent from one another. In both cases, separateness was understood as a necessary precursor of the valued qualities of civilization and reason.

In drawing these connections, I am not suggesting that Freud and Piaget were involved in a conspiracy to assert European superiority, nor am I suggesting that their work was driven by ideological commitments of which they were unaware. Rather, I am suggesting that since their work was indebted to the problems, terms and categories of 'level of development', their work was always prone to confirming the pertinence of those terms and categories even as they created new problems and sought new insights into development.

So how did level of development affect the value of children and childhood? In the late nineteenth and early twentieth centuries, children were understood as having a problematic relationship to separateness, to civilization and to reason. Ranking low on the scale of development, they were to be distinguished in value from 'primitives' and 'savages' only by their status as treasured possessions and, if they were male, as future civilized, reasoning individuals. To have high status in such societies meant living up to the standards of the time, that is to say living in pursuit of the qualities of separateness and independence. In short, with Freud and Piaget's help, separation became seen as a major source of human value. The semblance of separateness became an ideal gold standard of human value

Rejecting development: too much or too little separation?

Freud was genuinely concerned to understand taboo and law. By telling his readers about 'savages', he tried to tell them about themselves. Piaget did not want to condemn children as inferior but wanted to understand their thinking. Reading Freud and Piaget nowadays, however, one is struck by their use of such terms as 'savage' and 'primitive'. For a writer in the human sciences to use these words today would be simply unacceptable. No matter what precautions Freud and Piaget took to turn these words into neutral, technical terms, I cannot help but hear a fundamental tone of disrespect in them. These are words against dignity. In a sense, we can never read the 'same' books as Freud and Piaget's contemporaries did, because twentieth-century struggles against colonialism, sexism and racism have built on and altered the meanings of those words, making the oppression they once concealed clearly visible to all. In recent years even the word 'development' itself has been changing. The association forged by our grandparents' and great-grandparents' generations between level of development and the worth of humans has meant for some that to speak of 'child development' is to devalue children, to make it hard to think of them as anything but possessions. Thus, since the closing years of the twentieth century, many childhood researchers who are concerned with the question of the value of children and of childhood have responded critically to ideas of development and have distanced themselves from Freud and Piaget. This rejection takes two main forms: anti-developmental psychology and the new sociology of childhood.

Anti-developmental psychology (Stainton Rogers and Stainton Rogers 1992; Burman 1994; Morss 1996) begins with the insight that the independent individual that is so often taken for granted as the basis of society is not a natural phenomenon, but is primarily a political construct that serves the ideological function of justifying hierarchies of power and wealth. To go looking for the origins of this political construct in human instinct like Freud or in the laws of child development like Piaget is to mistake a social and political phenomenon for a natural one. When Piaget and Freud dwell on the importance of separateness they reveal their complicity with this ideology.

For sociologists of childhood, the problem is slightly different. By allowing that there are differences between adults and children, the developmental ideas of Freud and Piaget have provided a justification for ignoring differences between children. Each and every child is hidden behind the figure of the 'universal child' (James and Prout 1997; James et al. 1998) which conceals real children's individual, cultural and experiential differences. This universal child need have no wishes, desires and opinions of her own because her needs are already very well understood by experts on child development.

The difference between these responses on the issue of separateness is striking. Anti-developmental psychology is, generally speaking, opposed to a picture of adults as separate from and independent of each other. The sociology of childhood argues that we should recognize and respect the separateness of children one from another. On the one hand, there is the conviction that separateness is a fiction that distributes human value unfairly and which we should not believe in. On the other, there is an appreciation of the value that one loses when one is not understood as being separate.

As the principle of dignity inspires contemporary psychologists and sociologists to reject Freud and Piaget, an important difference has appeared between the disciplines. One way to give children their proper value is to reject the idea that adults are separate. Another way is to embrace the idea of separation for children. It seems that together these two very different responses to Freud and Piaget's work have captured an ambivalence that should be familiar to us from the previous chapter. This is the ambivalence that arises whenever actual and complete separation is the only tool available to us when we have to think about children's value.

As I argued in the previous chapter, there is a tendency for us to get stuck arguing about whether we want to see children and adults as separate or inseparable, when what we need to do is to acknowledge that sometimes separateness is positive and sometimes it is negative. In other words, if we are to be able to think clearly about relations between adults and children, we need to start recognizing just how conventional the categories we habitually use to create the value of adulthood and the value of childhood are, categories such as 'developed/primitive' and 'separate/attached'. To say that these categories are conventional, is not to imply that they are bad. It does not mean that we should reject them. But it does mean that we can have a little distance from them and give ourselves time and space to consider how to relate to them and even how to change them.

Conclusion

I began this chapter by exploring the importance of division and classification in the cultural creation of value. I argued that we can feel threatened when the categories we assume to be natural are shown to be conventional. I then gave some further examples of the creation of value by division. As I examined Taylor's distinction between societies of honour and those of dignity, I noted that where honour gave value by associating persons with the monarchy, dignity gives value on an individual basis to each and every person. This is a shift from building value by dividing categories of person to building value by dividing each person from every other so as to allow for assessment of their individual merits. Dignity needs separability. As 'level of development' bridged the gap between honour and dignity, however, it gave higher value to white European adult men than anyone else. Level of development gave high value to those who could claim independence from others.

If we wonder, as we did at the end of Chapter 1, why it is difficult for us to register a difference between separation and separability, the reasons for this should by now be clearer. 'Level of development' helped shape the world in the nineteenth century. It associated separation with high status. As I will show in greater detail in Part 2, we are still living with that equation. When the suggestion is made that children's status be altered from possession to self-possessor, that love needs to be accompanied by rights, we cannot imagine what that change might mean if it does not mean the actual and complete separation of children from those around them. Stated simply, our history has tangled some issues up for us. Is it possible for us to untangle them?

Fortunately for us, the long gap between the early and late twentieth century, between Freud and Piaget and the contemporary psychologists and sociologists who reject them, contains the work of many who were inspired by them but sought to differ from them. In Parts 3, 4 and 5, I will discuss the work of some of these authors, building a coherent picture of an alternative understanding of childhood that is based on separability rather than separation. This survey is intended to show just how we can untangle some of our historical knots and thus prepare ourselves to respond creatively to a world in which the conditions of childhood and adulthood are changing, rather than to react within that world. But first, even though I have examined the connections between separateness and value in the late nineteenth and early twentieth centuries, I have as yet offered little illustration of how these connections continued to be made in the mid and late twentieth centuries. So in the next part I will examine connections between childhood, social class and the performance of separation.

PART 2
SOCIAL STATUS AND PERFORMANCES OF SEPARATION

In Part 1, I described some contemporary distributions of children's value. I drew particular attention to an apparent conflict between ways of valuing children that deals with them primarily as possessions, and a way of valuing children that deals with them as individuals who are in possession of themselves. I argued that some people feel that the second way of valuing of children is ridiculous or even dangerous, particularly when it takes the form of children's rights to participate in decision-making as outlined in the Convention. I tried to explain these reactions by drawing a distinction between actual and complete separation of children from their carers, communities or cultures, and the quality of 'separability'. Separability is simply the possibility of children's temporary and partial separation from their carers, communities or cultures, the possibility that they might be considered for their own sake beyond the claims of those they otherwise 'belong' to. I argued that, broadly speaking, the reasons and feelings that underlie resistance to children's participatory rights are not bad reasons and feelings, but that they are misplaced. It may well be ridiculous or dangerous to expect children to make their minds up 'on their own' at all times and in all circumstances, but this is not the thrust of the main global children's rights instrument, the Convention. I argued that the Convention aims to build the quality of separability into the pattern of children's everyday lives, both to combat their abuse within possessive relationships and to strengthen those possessive bonds that are valuable and fruitful for adult and child alike.

Having made this case, I then tried to explain how it is that separation and separability are ever confused with one another. The explanation I offered drew on the argument that Western societies, developing over time through colonial, class and gender conflicts, came to distribute resources of social respect and personal dignity according to a scale of separateness or independence. The more independent one could appear, the more substantial as a person and the more noteworthy one was. I argued that this cultural tendency to give high status to those able to sustain a performance of separateness, be it a financial, emotional, cognitive or attitudinal performance, means that today's adult individuals often find themselves working towards or desirous of such independence. A history of conflict over status between groups including colonizers and colonized, men and women, bourgeois and labouring classes is written into many of our understandings of how to be a proper, valuable person. One result of this is that performances and statements of separateness and independence are often regarded as the most viable solution to the problems of status and self-worth that living in highly competitive societies can generate.

In essence, then, I argued that Western performances of personhood are shaped by an ideal of separateness. Though we all live in quite subtly differentiated and multi-faceted states of separability, having a wide variety of dependencies that we periodically recall and forget, draw on and disavow, the ideal of separation makes it very easy for us to think and feel in terms of the binary pair 'separate/dependent'. Thus, when changes in the shape and style of children's separability are suggested, we are inclined to imagine that actual and complete separation is on the agenda. If we hold to the ideal of separation, then we react accordingly. This does not mean that the motives behind reactionary responses to children's separability are always the same. For example, by rejecting children's separability, some will seek to spare children the presentational labour and emotional turmoil that can accompany the search for status through separateness. However, we can also imagine others who jealously guard what status they have generated for themselves as adults. Those who obsessively circle the unattainable goal of complete separateness might well resent any assistance given to children. They would view children as potential competitors.

As I developed this argument, however, it became clear to me that for it to be convincing, it was necessary not only to suppose that history has made it *possible* for us in our everyday lives to accept a strong connection between separation and high status, but that we are *in fact* inclined to make that association and to let it guide our thoughts and feelings. What reasons beyond the lessons of history are there to think that we are obliged to perform separateness? What features of contemporary society currently desensitize us to the subtleties of separability? To address these questions I now turn to the work of Bernstein (1971) and Beck (1992), two sociologists who have been closely concerned with the impression that the ideal of separation makes on our lives. By the end of Part 2, then, I should have drawn a clearer picture of what I mean by 'performances of separateness' and provided reasons to think that these performances continue to play an important part in everyday life.

3 Basil Bernstein
Language, class and separation

Introduction

Despite his reservations (Bernstein 2000), Basil Bernstein is often associated with a tradition of social theory and research known as socio-linguistics. This tradition compares the ways that different social groups use language. Bernstein began his research into language use by different socio-economic classes in England in the 1950s (Bernstein 1971), and continued refining his arguments throughout his life. His research programme pursued a well-defined core of propositions. He proposed that a particular linguistic 'code' dominates formal institutional life in England, that this code is more readily available to middle-class people than it is to working-class people, and that this difference can limit the educational achievement of working-class children. Crudely stated, Bernstein argues that since formal institutions, including schools, tend to 'speak a different language' than working-class people, socio-economic class structures tend to be reproduced generation after generation. For Bernstein, the term 'working class' included semi-skilled and unskilled workers who lacked education or training beyond obligatory schooling.

By the early 1970s Bernstein's work had begun to attract criticism. Bernstein (2000) cites Labov (1977) as a prominent critic. Labov took the view that Bernstein had judged working-class people to be linguistically *deficient*. He argued that this understanding of the disadvantaged was unlikely to help them and was quite likely further to damage them and their life chances. To be characterized as 'deficient' often means losing the respect of the powerful in society and such characterization also has the potential to degrade one's own self-respect. Bernstein's critics tended to prefer to judge the language use of the disadvantaged as *different* from but equally as valid as existing standards, rather than as *deficient* with respect to those standards. Labov (1977), for example, attempted to tackle the idea, prevalent in the United States of his day, that African-Americans were being held back economically by their use of a logically inferior dialect of English. Labov convincingly argued that despite many non-standard grammatical features, such as the regular use of double negatives, Black English Vernacular was just as capable of expressing complex logical relationships as 'standard' English. He made this argument to establish that since Black English Vernacular was different and not deficient, there must be other reasons for African-Americans' economic disadvantages. The high political stakes of this deficiency/difference argument become clear when we realize that characterizing the disadvantaged as deficient can obscure other possible accounts of their disadvantage. By dismissing the deficiency view, Labov's (1977) work made space for the consideration of racism as a factor in reproducing African-Americans' disadvantage.

This controversy of the 1970s was to a large extent about the degree of respect that Bernstein was understood to have for the disadvantaged. His critics believed that if academic researchers saw the disadvantaged as different rather than as deficient, greater respect for and understanding of the disadvantaged would be generated in society. This belief may or may not have been well founded. However, as I will argue, Bernstein himself was not principally concerned with making respectful or disrespectful judgements of different linguistic 'codes' and different social groups; rather, he was examining the role that linguistic 'codes' play in the distribution of opportunity and respect among persons in society. His intention as a sociologist was not to judge, but to observe what judgements are made and how they are made, not to distribute opportunity, but to observe and understand the means by which it is distributed.

As I describe Bernstein's (1971) project, it should become clear just how sensitive he was to the performance of separateness and its relationship to social status and respect. I would like you to consider Bernstein's work as evidence for my claim that an ideal of separateness does in fact shape our lives and is therefore capable of shaping our thinking and feeling about the value of children and of childhood. By the end of the chapter I should also have made the concept of separability a good deal clearer by reinterpreting Bernstein's findings for my current purposes. Before we turn to these issues, however, I need first to describe two kinds of background to Bernstein's work. In the next two sections, I will provide a sketch of the relevant aspects of the English education system of the mid-1950s and of the sociological background that Bernstein drew on in studying that system.

Education and social class

Bernstein (1971) began his research into relationships between linguistic codes and social class in the context of the English education system of the mid-1950s. At that time, state-funded provision for children over the age of 11 came in two broad kinds (see Jones, 2003, for a thorough account). The curricula at boys' 'grammar' and girls' 'high' schools were designed to educate a future socio-economic middle class. The middle classes of the 1950s were distinguished from the working classes by their relatively well-paid, secure and high status employment and by their taste for 'high' culture such as 'classical' rather than 'popular' music and 'literary' novels rather than genre fiction about crime, cowboys and romance (Hoggart 1958). A middle-class education encouraged those intellectual skills associated with high status, professional occupations, such as a familiarity with Latin, and the cultivation of high status tastes for music and literature among their pupils. A quite different type of education was on offer in the 'secondary modern' schools (Bernstein 1971: 30). Curricula here were geared toward vocational training for future skilled and unskilled manual labourers. The development of pupils' literacy was geared toward creating functional workers rather than toward broadening horizons and cultivating sensibilities. Woodwork and metalwork training, provided alongside English and Maths, would provide the basic skill base for future builders, plumbers, mechanics and unskilled manual labourers.

Children were channelled into one side or other of the institutional division of social classes and curricula partly on the basis of their scores in examinations taken at the end of primary education, at around age 11. The examination, often referred to as the 'eleven plus', was open to all children, regardless of their social class. The children, it seemed, were being treated equally. The level ground of the examination would give them equal opportunities to gain access to schools that would prepare them for well-paid, high status, middle-class careers. Indeed, one of the principal motivations of the progressive politicians who shaped the education system in England in the years after the Second World War was to ensure that it distributed opportunity fairly and gave each child an education that was suited to their aptitudes (Jones 2003). Given this background, it was quite surprising that the type of secondary school that children were channelled into reflected, more often than not, the class positions of their parents. In a situation of apparently equal opportunities, outcomes for children remained unequal. How could this be accounted for?

Accounting for class structure

As we have seen, the English education system of the 1950s offered an apparent equality of opportunity, but still tended to reproduce existing class structure and inequalities of outcome. It is quite possible to take the view that the inequalities of outcome reflected fundamental inequalities of ability in children of different social classes. On this view, the relatively low performance of lower-class children in the eleven plus exams was a result of their lesser ability, and their secondary school destinations accurately reflected this lesser ability. If we accept this account, then it is clear that secondary education was doing a good job, channelling each child into a social position that he or she was suited to. This account provides us with a ready explanation of the reproduction of the two main social classes over generations – social classes are merely a large-scale expression of differences between individuals, some of whom are more able than others. If a few lower-class children of the 1950s found their way into grammar school, then they were the exception that proved the rule. The meritocratic mechanism of the eleven plus exam had detected their unusual talent and rescued them from the accident of their background.

As I described this first account of the reproduction of social classes, it may have reminded you of other accounts of inequality that we have encountered so far in other contexts. This is because the idea that inequalities between social groups simply reflect the abilities of the individuals that constitute those groups has been used to account for inequalities between classes, genders and ethnicities for many years. The deficiency view of US ethnic inequality criticized by Labov (1977) is a variant of this account. As we saw in Chapter 2, it also formed a vital part of the discrimination among genders, ethnicities, social classes and age groups on the basis of 'level of development'. Even though it is a controversial way of accounting for inequalities of outcome and for the production of broad classes and status groups, it still has its proponents. It is not so long since Herrnstein and Murray (1994) argued that the contemporary economic position of African-Americans is a direct result of their individual intellectual deficiencies. We might not be comfortable with this sort of account, but it would certainly seem to explain societal divisions. It often seems difficult to provide an alternative. As long as we think of social classes as the simple accumulation of individuals of comparable inherent ability, this account will have all the persuasive force of common sense. As Jones (2003) points out, this account certainly passed for common sense among many politicians and educational policy-makers of the 1940s and 1950s.

Even though Labov (1977) detected elements of the deficiency view in his work, Bernstein's common sense was quite different from that described above. The key to understanding Bernstein and the challenge he presented to 1950s' schooling lies in his *sociological* approach to the issue of class and inequality. As we have seen, the deficiency view of class structure explains large-scale features of society, such as the division of classes, as the result of the simple gathering together of individuals of differing ability. On this view, small-scale differences in the ability of individuals lead to the large-scale phenomenon of class. In contrast, despite their many differences, sociological accounts of class division all tend to explain it as the result of processes that have the power to select, channel and direct individuals to class positions with little regard for their individual abilities. Two quite different sociologists, Marx (Marx and Engels 1998) and Durkheim (1984), illustrate this distinctive sociological approach very well.

Sociological approaches to class structure

Displaying remarkable intellectual ambition, Marx (Marx and Engels 1998) argued that the whole of human history should be interpreted as an ongoing conflict between two main social groups. Whether he was discussing ancient Roman citizens and the slaves they owned, medieval nobles and the peasants they governed, or factory owners and the workers they employed, Marx insisted that what objectively distinguished exploiters from the exploited was one thing and one thing only – whether or not they owned the 'means of production'. A slave was owned by and worked land that was owned by a citizen. A peasant owed agricultural labour to the noble who owned the land they lived on. Industrial workers saw little of the profit their labour generated because ownership of the factory gave their employer the upper hand in crucial negotiations about pay and conditions. In each case, the basic nature of the relationship between exploiter and exploited has nothing to do with the abilities of the individuals concerned. Whether or not an individual of the dominant class was highly intelligent, crafty or diligent, they owned the means of production and were therefore in a position of power and high status. Idleness, stupidity and poor character might disadvantage this individual in their relationships with peers, but not in their relationships with their economic inferiors. In Marx's sociology, individual ability, whether 'deficient' or 'different', had very little to do with one's fundamental social position. Class structure is defined by ownership not by ability.

A central feature of Durkheim's (1984) work was a refusal to begin the task of explaining sociological phenomena at the level of the individual person. For him, there was no question of large-scale social phenomena, like social class, being accounted for by small-scale issues like the innate qualities of individuals. The task of the sociologist was not primarily to explain how a single person found themselves in a given occupational class, but first to understand why Western industrial societies were composed of such classes in the first place. Durkheim, then, asked questions about the 'division of labour' between classes and how it arose. Like Marx, Durkheim's ambition was to address the division of labour throughout human history.

Durkheim argued that over the course of human history, one great social development can be observed. This development is a change in the way that the tasks that allow people to be fed, clothed and educated, the tasks necessary for society's maintenance, are distributed among persons. He began by arguing that early in human history, population density was low. This meant both that natural resources were relatively abundant and that a high degree of self-sufficiency was essential to survival. Under these conditions, 'society' had certain characteristics. It was composed of many relatively small, relatively independent family groups. All the main skills for the production of the goods and tools necessary for survival and for the reproduction of the next generation could be found in each such group. The groups were largely independent of each other in practical terms because the skills necessary for the maintenance of life and the continuance of society were represented within each group. For my purposes, the key feature of this style of division of labour is that each person is involved in many types of work on a daily basis. The list of different types of work performed by one person might include child-care, hunting, trapping, medicine, starting a fire, building accommodation and finding good water. In these circumstances there was relatively little specialization.

If such an unspecialized society prospered, population density would rise. In consequence, natural resources would become less abundant and high degrees of self-sufficiency would be unnecessary. With increasing population density, a threshold would arise at which the old style of division of labour would become less efficient than a new style, based on specialization. For example, if one group of people specialized in baking bread, and if they exchanged their bread with groups that had other specialities, they would be able to use the economies of scale involved in baking for everybody to refine and to elaborate their bread-making skills. This would help to secure their claim on expertise and to compete effectively with other claimants to their special role. For Durkheim, then, increases in population density led to the evolution of more complex and differentiated societies characterized by practical interdependence between occupational groups. A key feature of these societies is their use of well-defined occupational roles to narrow and sharpen specialisms so as to maximize the efficiency of exploitation of natural resources.

In Durkheim's (1984) view, modern Western societies were societies of this second, complex and differentiated type. On this basis it is easy to see the social classes of such societies as ours as the product of particular divisions of labour, the outcome of a societal response to a history of increasing population density, rather than as a reflection of the innate qualities of individuals. This is because as long as the necessary occupational roles are filled, and as long as these roles are well coordinated, the innate abilities of the individuals who fill them are largely irrelevant, given some very basic level of competence. In a highly role-differentiated society, most individuals would arrive at a social position not through some objective test of their aptitudes and abilities, but through a social mechanism that gave them access to that role. Family inheritance is a traditional social mechanism of this kind. One generation of bakers gives rise to another, and the reputation of the family as specialists in baking opens doors for the next generation. In contemporary societies, however, where family name and reputation do not always carry very far, this mechanism has been supplemented by education oriented toward the attainment of qualifications.

Language and intelligence

Now that I have sketched both the social and sociological contexts that informed Bernstein, I can begin to describe his work in more detail. As a sociologist with some experience of educating young people, Bernstein's interest was piqued by the role that schooling seemed to be playing in the reproduction of class structure. The studies of class and the division of labour conducted by Marx (Marx and Engels 1998) and Durkheim (1984) provided him with good reasons to reject the idea that class structure is the result of the unfolding of the innate abilites of different sections of the population. As we have seen, Durkheim's account was that occupational class structure was produced and reproduced by the distinctly social processes of organization. If this account held any value, then the English education system might provide an ideal site to investigate these processes. Bernstein (1971) reported some interesting data he had gathered on this topic.

Bernstein had taken a group of 309 male, working-class 'day release' students. They were all 'messenger boys', 16- and 17-year-old trainee postmen employed by the Post Office, who were released for a day each week to attend classes. They were all based in London and came from unskilled or semi-skilled backgrounds. Some 295 of them had attended secondary modern schools, the 14 remaining having attended junior technical, central or grammar schools. Bernstein gave his participant group two different tests of cognitive ability, both of which could deliver a single figure assessment of the participants' intelligence quotients or IQs. One test, the 'Progressive Matrices 1938' tested IQ by posing a series of 'non-linguistic relational problems involving logical addition and subtraction' (Bernstein 1971: 32). The other, the 'Mill Hill vocabulary test 1948' tested IQ through 'purely linguistic problems of a conceptual or categorizing order'. Significantly, the tests differed in how much emphasis they gave to language use.

Nowadays, IQ tests, though still widely used, are controversial. Some scientists are suspicious of the notion of innate traits of intelligence in individuals, preferring to think of intelligence as a set of skills that can change with practice and across contexts (Lewontin et al. 1985). Bernstein's use of these tests, however, did not rely on their ability accurately to measure the boys' intelligence. His central concern was not to find out how clever or dull these boys were. Instead, he was interested in whether the scores from the two different tests displayed a similar pattern.

Given that the tests were both designed to measure the same property (IQ), when the results are charted, we might expect to see two lines on the graph that more or less follow each other. The higher a boy's non-linguistic IQ score, the higher his linguistic IQ score ought to be. Both scores should vary between boys in roughly the same way because each boy should score roughly the same in both tests. Before administering the tests and collating the results, however, Bernstein predicted that the lines would diverge from each other. Specifically, he predicted that the higher the result a boy achieved in the non-linguistic test, the greater the difference would be between his two test results. In other words, Bernstein predicted that even as the non-linguistic IQ line rose, the linguistic IQ line would remain relatively flat. Bernstein's prediction proved to be accurate. A given boy's high score in the non-linguistic test could not be relied upon to predict a high score in the linguistic test. This was because, whatever their measured non-linguistic IQ, the linguistic performance of all of these lower-class boys was mediocre. This was an interesting result indeed, but what did it have to do with class and education? How could it help Bernstein to identify those social processes taking place within the education system that might contribute to the reproduction of social class? The disparity between the two sets of IQ results gave Bernstein reason to pursue the idea that particular ways of using language was of central importance. It is from this starting point that Bernstein developed his explanation of how schooling helped to reproduce class structure.

Public language

Bernstein had already developed a model of differences in language use between lower- and middle-class people. There was a history of research in this area that helped him formulate his prediction about the boys' performance. Bernstein cites studies which found that working-class children tended to use a higher percentage of nouns, less complicated sentences, to ask fewer questions and to use more exclamations than their middle-class peers. This gave an impression of a style of language use that was oriented toward things and people rather than qualities and characteristics, toward forceful and immediate expression and away from the qualification of statements and attempts to gather more information. Bernstein refined and elaborated this early impression. He argued that as well as having the orientation that earlier studies had detected, working-class people tended to express themselves as if they were selecting their utterances from a publicly available code, what he termed a 'public language'. In later research, Bernstein often referred to this as a 'restricted code' for reasons that will become clear. The general lack of qualification in utterances was connected, in Bernstein's view, with a style of language use in which individuals did not mark their statements as originating from their own unique thought processes. Thus, instead of being a vehicle for expressing individuality, it was a vehicle for expressing a community of mutual understanding. For Bernstein, the mediocre performance of his participants in language-based tests of intelligence, consistently exhibited despite variations in their non-linguistic IQ test, is a result of their reliance on public language and working-class use of public language partly accounts for the reproduction of social class divisions through schooling.

We might normally think of all spoken utterances as originating within the private space of the individual mind. Indeed, as Derrida (1976) has argued, this picture of language use has such common-sense appeal that it shaped the theory of language developed by de Saussure (1960), the founder of modern linguistics. However, not all language use is like this. Spoken language is a very versatile technology. For example, in the highly specialized environment of a medical operating theatre, when a surgeon requests a piece of equipment, she is unlikely to say 'I think I need a scalpel' – the word 'scalpel' suffices. Our surgeon, then, is not using language to express her private, inner thoughts, but is making a selection from a routine set of possibilities, a code understood by all theatre staff, that unambiguously identifies each surgical tool without the need for further elaboration. For Bernstein, English working-class people tended to use language in a similar way to the surgeon, selecting from a range of options in the assumption that this range is understood by all. The difference between the high status surgeon and the working-class speaker is that the surgeon reserves this code, this way of using language, for specific situations, while the lower-class speaker uses such a code in many everyday circumstances.

Let us consider some of the examples of the linguistic code 'public language' that Bernstein provides.

> Mother to child on bus: 'Hold on tight.' Child: 'Why?' Mother: 'Hold on *tight!*' Child: 'Why?' Mother: 'I told you to hold on tight, didn't I?'

> Father to son: 'You're not going out.' Son: 'Why can't I go?' Father: 'I told you, you're not going out. Now shut up!'

> (1971: 57)

With these examples Bernstein is arguing that, as a code, the public language used by English working classes resists elaboration. As the children ask their questions, a statement is repeated as if its content alone should suffice. When the children ask again, it is forcefully pointed out to them that the relevant statement has been made. Neither a chain of reasoning nor a report of the parents' feelings and intentions is summoned. If these are examples of 'public language', we can see that it is 'public' in the sense that speakers feel that the meaning of their utterances should be immediately obvious to all and should therefore require no further elaboration. Once spoken, the words are 'out there', floating full of meaning in the air and there is no need to refer them back to their source. Further, in their self-evident completeness, the utterances of public language are unrelated one to another. Utterances are treated as if they were discrete objects, not as if they were elements of an interconnected pattern of ideas, feelings and relationships. One can, perhaps, sense the parents' frustration that their children have failed to be impressed by their utterances. Are their children stupid or just wilful that they do not recognize what is available for all to see? One can also imagine that for the children concerned, asking questions can come to seem as much to do with making a risky challenge to authority as with seeking explanation. In public language, reasons for a given course of action can become confounded with the authority of the speaker. The question 'why?' can be answered with 'because I said so' and that answer can be backed up with a declaration of authority such as 'because I am your father'.

Bernstein's public language has other interesting characteristics. It will include statements that take the form of questions such as 'It's only natural, isn't it?' as if the speaker were involving their listener and assuming their listener's agreement from the outset. It will also involve the individual speaker in selecting from a group of 'idiomatic phrases'. What Bernstein seems to have in mind here is the use of popular catchphrases and turns of speech. Bernstein provides few examples of these, but were he alive today, he might have noticed the contemporary use, in the UK, of the phrase 'like you do' to punctuate anecdotes, and the circulation of linguistic tics drawn from popular television programmes ('don't even go there', 'that is sooo not true'). Each of these in its own way presumes upon a common understanding between speaker and listener. 'Like you do' invokes shared assumptions of normal conduct, and, if the anecdote involves comical or extraordinary events and reactions, can be used wryly. Turns of phrase drawn from television programmes evoke a common experience of viewing. As you may have noticed from these examples, the use of the public language code is in no way restricted to lower socio-economic classes. Wherever friends, acquaintances and colleagues meet and feel able to participate in a warm, enjoyable conversational exchange, the signs of public language use can be detected. In many circumstances it is either safe to assume that there is a common ground of understanding or to assume that interlocutors will cooperate in an attempt to generate common ground. As Bernstein notes, public language is a code of community. It can be used in relaxation, in socializing, in play and to humanize interaction in work environments. Why, then, the association between the public language code and working-class people?

Formal language and humiliation

For Bernstein, working-class English people were not distinguished from middle-class people by exclusive use of public language. The difference between the groups that Bernstein used to account for the reproduction of class structure through the education system, was that middle-class speakers also had access to a second code that he called 'formal language'. The key characteristic of formal language is that speakers do not necessarily rely on or attempt to generate common ground with their audience. Rather than select utterances as if from a common pool, speakers mark their utterances as their own, as emanating from their individual thought processes. As Bernstein puts it, 'A critical difference between the two speech forms is that whereas in a *formal* language subjective intent may be verbally elaborated and made explicit, this process is not facilitated in a *public* language' (1971: 47).

Formal language tends to signal the individual authorship of utterances. In this way, individuals become responsible for their utterances. If listeners feel a need for further detail or clarification of a statement or request, they can reasonably ask the speaker to say more. Rather than being treated as the common property of all, spoken words are related to individual persons and may be referred back to them. A number of consequences arise from this key characteristic of formal language. Since utterances are taken to originate within the privacy of the individual mind, formal code use involves the assumption that more meaning may lie behind the words. This supplementary meaning may be sought by asking questions that take what has already been said into account. Thus, if asked a question, formal language users are under some obligation to elaborate. If they fail to elaborate, they risk being seen as excessively sparing in their speech. For example, a failure to elaborate on reasons may lead to a perception that they are unreasonable, that they have no justification for what they have said. Likewise, a failure to elaborate on intentions and feelings may lead to a perception that they are hiding something, or are confused or ashamed of themselves.

From the fundamental relationship between individuals and their utterances that is established within the code, from the obligation that this relationship enshrines, a general tendency emerges to see the world in terms of relationships and differentiated qualities. This has particularly important consequences when a speaker is in a position of authority. I noted above how public language allowed for the justification of statements by reference to authority. If formal language speakers are obliged to remain open to elaboration, it is clear that formal language speakers who are in positions of authority might try to avoid ending discussions by simple reference to their authority. In formal language, authority must be justified with reasons. This places persons with authority in an interesting position. To wield authority and to remain consistent with the requirements of formal language, they must split themselves in two. Such a person's social or institutional position may lend them authority, but they must also be able to stand to one side of it so that they may justify it through reason.

As I have suggested, on Bernstein's view, while middle-class people have access to both formal and public language, working-class people tend to have less easy access to formal language. If working-class people were never obliged to spend time in social contexts that take familiarity with formal language for granted, this difference would only be a socio-linguistic curiosity. However, education is obligatory in England and schools make extensive use of formal language both within the curriculum, where lessons often focus on elaborating reason, and in inter-personal interaction, as when a teacher addresses a pupil. When schools demand that their pupils be individually responsible for their words and deeds, when this is seen as the foundation of good character, formal code is clearly required. On Bernstein's view, class difference in code usage lays the foundations for working-class children's bad experience of school and schools' bad experience of working-class children.

The mismatch between the institutional norm of formal language and working-class pupils' use of public language affects the perceptions teachers have of pupils and pupils of teachers. It has consequences for the fundamental matter of trust between pupils and teachers. Imagine that a teacher, using formal language, asks a public language-speaking pupil a question. For this pupil, asking questions is closely related to challenging authority. Being asked a question in full view of his peers has already disturbed him slightly. He gives a brief answer. The teacher requests elaboration. The pupil doesn't know what to say because he has already given his answer. It seems likely to him that the teacher is trying to make a fool of him. If his answer wasn't satisfactory, then it must have been wrong, but the teacher has not told him outright that it is wrong. The teacher must be toying with him. He might repeat his answer, word for word, or point out that he has answered already and risk appearing to defy the teacher. He might say nothing. He might mumble that he doesn't know. Either way, the pupil is certainly discomfited and possibly humiliated. For his own part, the teacher may be used to seeing pupils perform like this and 'give up' when asked questions. To him these pupils might seem lazy. But the pupil does not realize that as far the teacher is concerned asking a question is very far from acting in an insulting way. He does not realize that from the teacher's perspective he has an obligation to elaborate if asked for elaboration. This may make the pupil appear stupid in the teacher's eyes. The overall result is that the pupil gathers a history of humiliating encounters with teachers, while the teacher's expectations of this pupil are gradually lowered. All this follows from the extensive use of formal code in educational contexts.

Codes and the erosion of trust

Feelings of humiliation and perceptions of laziness will clearly have their effects on the level of trust in the classroom. When the two codes meet, trust is also put under more direct pressure. This is because the two codes embody quite different understandings of what a person should be faithful to when they speak. They imply different models of honesty and personal integrity. Public language demands a 'straightforward' approach to interaction, an approach that displays fidelity to the expectations of the audience. Trust is based on a commitment to one's listeners to respect their assumption that once something has been said, it has been fully exposed and made available for all to see. Against this backdrop, elaboration is positively dangerous because it can be difficult for one's listeners to tell the difference between qualifying a statement and contradicting that statement or being evasive. Let us take an example. Imagine that a public language speaker is asked whether she enjoyed a movie. She asserts the view that the movie was 'rubbish'. Others disagree and say they quite enjoyed it. This might turn into a lively exchange. It might even become heated. Tension can be diffused by a participant using a stock phrase like 'each to their own' or 'everyone is entitled to their opinion'. A difference of opinion may persist, the opinions floating in the air, unrelated to each other except by their antagonism. The difference of opinion may even form the basis of a lasting personal resentment. None of the participants, however, has shown themselves to be untrustworthy. Each has simply 'stood their ground'. Interactions of this kind can be found in groups, regardless of social class. They emerge as a consequence of the adoption of public language, and, as we have seen, public language is available to all speakers.

If our movie-goer replied to the question in formal code, however, the interaction may take on a rather different form. Formal code would not normally admit an outright, emotive denunciation of the film. Depending on her sensitivity to the expectations of her interlocutors, a speaker who is comfortable with both public and formal language has a number of options. She may dive in with a public language style of response and potentially encounter blunt rebuttal. She may try to strike a balance, crafting a brief reply that signals that she is reporting on her feelings rather than on the film itself, saying 'It's not my sort of thing really'. This would make it clear that her response reflects her individual relationship to the film. In doing so, she would be fulfilling the formal code obligation to be responsible for her utterances, but she would also limit the risk of elaboration. This might lead others to see her as aloof. They may wonder why she is not telling them whether she thought the film was good or not. Alternatively she could go into greater depth about her response to the film. She could describe how, at first, she was hostile to it, later found merit in certain sequences, was even able to appreciate one actor's performance but, in the end, was disappointed and felt that the director had not served the story well. The issue that divides the codes here is whether her interlocutors hear this nuanced report as a full and balanced answer, or as an evasion of the question. It qualifies and adds details. It makes exceptions and admits of a mixture of feelings. It does not deliver a 'straightforward' answer because it allows that there may be more to come in the way of response. By being faithful to her responsibilities within formal code, she alienates her interlocutors. They might even think she is trying to 'show off' or that she is taking the film too seriously when it was only an entertainment. If it is pointed out to her that she has not answered the question, she may be irritated because, in her view, she has.

It is clear from the movie example just how the mismatch of codes can erode trust. What passes for integrity in public language – 'standing your ground' – looks like obstinacy from a formal perspective. Likewise, the formal integrity of admitting a complex, personalized and highly distinctive account can look like evasion or self-contradiction from the public perspective. In a group of acquaintances these issues have consequences for participants' perceptions of each other and of themselves as group members. Obstinacy is a failure to respect the individuality of others in the group. Evasion can suggest that others are not to be trusted with a direct response or are beneath the speaker's level. The mismatch means that all participants are exposed to potential insult, either in the form of rudeness or snobbery. Let us now reconsider how this mismatch may unfold in a school setting, bearing in mind Bernstein's view that differences in code use underlie class differences in educational pathways and career outcome.

Codes, trust and moral worlds

As well as teaching to curricula, schools punish children. In Bernstein's day, children were beaten in English schools, often with a special implement such as a cane. Beatings were understood to help maintain the everyday order of the school. Beatings were also understood, somewhat ironically from a contemporary perspective, to play a part in teaching children the difference between right and wrong. Other punishments, which served the same dual purpose of enforcing order and the difference between right and wrong, included 'detention' and 'lines'. In detention, children lost scheduled free time – breaks or a lunch hour – or were held back after the end of the school day. Thus, to encourage children in their school career, more 'school' was given as punishment. Similarly, 'lines' exaggerated and perverted a normal classroom activity to produce a punitive effect. If children displayed inattention to their schoolwork, which often consisted of repetitive writing exercises, they could be instructed to carry out further writing exercises such as copying from a book or writing many repetitions of an improving phrase. As I have noted, these punishments were sometimes understood as a way of modifying children's behaviour away from what was 'wrong' and toward what was 'right', the assumption being that children misbehaved because they did not know the difference between right and wrong. It is remarkable that school authorities conducted themselves as if children's obedience were identical to 'right' behaviour and as if children had no moral insights of their own. As I will suggest in the following illustration, children did have their own moral insights, these were of a piece with linguistic code, and the way their insights interacted with school authority could have a profound effect on their perceptions of the value of schooling and on their career choices.

Imagine that a teacher has an especially punitive attitude. Week after week, pupils find themselves in detention during the lunch break that follows this teacher's lesson. Since the teacher adopts the jurisprudential assumption of collective class responsibility, normal in English schools at least in Bernstein's day, many pupils who have not done anything 'wrong' find themselves detained alongside those who have. They feel that this is not fair and decide to make a complaint to another teacher. Let us assume that this second teacher does not immediately endorse the aggrieved pupils' view. The second teacher's range of responses to this complaint are shaped by our two linguistic codes. She may respond to their complaint through public language, and simply re-assert the fact of authority by telling them that 'life's not fair'. In doing so she brings an end to the conversation. Once 'life' as a whole is announced as 'not fair', no further explanation or elaboration is necessary, or indeed worthwhile. The pupils can, as the phrase has it, 'like it or lump it' because, within the terms of reference of public language, teachers, rather than being individuals who have a relationship to their own authority, simply embody authority.

What happens if the teacher adopts formal language? Once again, let us assume that she does not immediately endorse the aggrieved pupils' view. In this case, she may accept that the pupils are unhappy with the situation. She will explain, however, that it would be unwise for her to make judgements about another teacher's disciplinary practices. After all, she cannot know the full details because she was not in the class himself. As a teacher she knows that it is sometimes necessary to do things that seem unfair and that sometimes there is no better alternative. If she feels a need to explain to the pupils why she is not going to act on their behalf, she might say that though she has sympathy for their position, it is important for teachers to stick together, because without teacherly solidarity, school discipline as a whole would collapse. Now that I have described the situation and two of its possible outcomes, I can use it to illustrate the relationship between the codes and the pupils' moral worlds.

The first point to notice is that, whatever code she adopts, the practical content of the second teacher's response is the same. The issue of fairness will be taken no further. But although the two versions amount to much the same thing, they are distinguished by code and by degree of elaboration. Significantly, this distinction can only be appreciated by those who are comfortable both with public and formal codes. Imagine that the pupils are middle class and, in Bernstein's terms, familiar both with public and formal language. How would they react to the two different versions? Presented with the public language response, depending on the teacher's demeanour, they might laugh and accept that this second teacher, at least, is a decent person. If the teacher is less charming, however, they may form a negative opinion of her, thinking her ignorant, and take their complaint elsewhere. Presented with the formal response, as people who are familiar with formal code, they will understand that they are being given more than a simple assertion of life's moral limitations. They will notice that the teacher acknowledges the feelings that underlie their complaint. They may feel that in offering them an explanation she is offering them some respect as individuals who happen to be pupils. Further, they will notice that the teacher is telling them, as a person distinct from her teacherly role, that her role imposes constraints on her actions and that she must accept these constraints because they are part of a web of relationships that supports the school as a whole. Even though their situation has not changed, the pupils may feel that they have learned something about the way the institution works. This understanding can help bind them to the school since it allows them to read a long-term purpose into what is otherwise just a repetition of the original injustice. The second teacher's support of the first teacher is not simply wrong, it is instrumental in supporting the functions of the school. Formal language has helped to make an injustice appear temporary and palatable.

Let us now consider the possible reactions of pupils who are comfortable only with public language. They too might laugh when told that life is not fair. If the second teacher lacks humour and charm, they might, on reflection, still appreciate what she has said. She has, after all, been straightforward and honest. This, if not exactly just, is trustworthy. They might tell each other that 'you know where you are' with the second teacher. If the second teacher offers them an elaborated formal language response, however, it is likely that the outcome will be negative. From the perspective of public language, the teacher's elaborations could appear weak, confused, self-serving or even hypocritical. Since teachers *are* authority rather than individuals in a relationship with authority, the second teacher's failure to use her authority is confusing. Perhaps she is frightened of the other teacher. If the second teacher does not declare that the punishment is right or wrong in a straightforward manner, she must be confused, dithering, perhaps cowardly. The pupils might notice that at first she says they are right but then says she is not going to do anything about it. That means, at least, that she has contradicted herself and, perhaps, that she is a hypocrite. They are being given a disrespectful 'bullshit' response. The teacher's careful elaboration of her complex and divided position is nothing more than double-talk and she is a person of little integrity. On this basis it would be quite understandable if the pupils felt morally disgusted. They might conclude that formal institutions such as their school are run by and produce morally diminished people. They are certainly not the first observers to take this view of institutional life, nor will they be the last.

Summary

We are now in a position to summarize the potential effects of the public/ formal code distinction on the school experience and career outcomes of working-class pupils. When a pupil is unable to respond in formal code to a question posed in formal code, she may appear stupid or lazy to the teacher. This pupil, for her own part, may be confused by the teacher's questions and may feel humiliated, having failed at a task she did not understand. The teacher might form a low opinion of this pupil's ability. The pupil may feel a need to repair her self-respect. Her peers may have a similar experience of school. They are able to communicate with one another highly effectively through public language and may generate great solidarity with each other in opposition to the values of the school. The anti-school sub-culture that may form will be based on the maintenance of a clear moral identity that opposes 'bullshit' and demands a 'straightforward' manner. Pupils will be willing to treat conflict with their peers as an opportunity to demonstrate their ability to stand their ground. In the longer term the pupil may develop an antipathy toward authority and a reluctance to wield authority for fear of becoming morally diminished. If we add these factors to the challenging nature of the eleven plus examination, it is clear that, in Bernstein's day at least, schooling could function as a key element in the maintenance of a division of labour between classes. As it recreates different occupational classes, it is able to ignore individual ability and, instead, channel pupils on the basis of class membership as signified by their language practices. The difference between working-class and middle-class children is not one of intellectual ability but one of value carried within linguistic codes. Working-class pupils operate according to different values than those that are supported within the school. They are therefore treated as less valuable than other children. This low valuation of working-class children extends into their later careers where, unless succesfully self-employed in a 'trade' like plumbing or bricklaying, they become low paid and expendable pairs of hands. We can now understand just how linguistic code affects educational outcomes. But what relevance does this have for my argument about separateness and separability?

Conclusion

I have remarked on the tendency of public language to presume upon or to create common understanding. By drawing on stock phrases and by seeking to confirm the expectations an audience has of a speaker to hold nothing back, the public language speakers minimize the difference between their point of view and that of their audience. Thus, in public language there are many exclamations but few surprises. Public language embeds its users in a community of understanding, while limiting their appreciation that the world may be understood otherwise. With a single, readily confirmed outlook on the world to hand, there is no need for elaboration, nuance, extensive reasoning or emotional reserve. The key distinguishing feature of formal language, however, is that it signals that utterances come from a particular place – the individual and private mind of the speaker. Formal language maximizes the potential difference between speakers' points of view and that of their audience. As a conversation proceeds and the relevant points of view are elaborated, it may become apparent that they are shared. But sharing a point of view is neither a necessary basis for nor a necessary outcome of conversation. Public language creates a community united in the face of a simple world of objects and events. Formal language creates individuals who have multiple, negotiable relationships. Summarizing the two codes in this way makes it clear that public language can be read as a strategy of connection while formal language can be read as a strategy of separation. Indeed, from the point of view of a public language, the main result of formal language is to make its users cold, distant and untrustworthy. On this view, it would seem that I could map public and formal language directly onto an apparent conflict I examined in Chapter 1. When 'love' and 'rights' are brought together in conflict, the concern is that cold, legalistic, formal rights will dissolve the mysterious and essentially inarticulable bonds of 'love' between generations. What code would monstrous rights-bearing children speak once they had dispensed with the predictable clichés of 'love', except for a precocious formality? But to accept this is to accept the judgement of those who would like to keep the world simple. Bernstein has more to offer.

Recall that Bernstein does not map public language onto the working class and formal language onto the middle class. The difference between the two classes was not their exclusive ownership of different codes, but the degree to which they were comfortable with both codes. Just because an individual uses formal language on some occasions does not mean that they never use public language. From the point of view of someone fluent in both codes, there might be no antagonism between them. Instead, they might simply be suited to different purposes. In some relationships, warmth, community and relative inarticulacy might be appropriate. In others, a more reserved and circumspect performance may be required. From this point of view, linguistic codes are not possessions but performances. Although many, more formal, parts of life require formal, individualized performances, not all of life is like this. It does happen to be the case, however, that many of the moments in which wealth and status are distributed, such as exams and job interviews, require formal language performances, performances of separation.

I illustrated above how language codes are closely tied to emotional responses and to moral judgements. Humiliation and disgust are part of institutional life. If some pupils can operate both language codes, issues of emotion and morality give yet another spin to the matter of middle-class advantage. Middle-class pupils are advantaged not simply by their familiarity with formal language but by their knowledge that it is possible to move between codes, to change track when it seems appropriate. Just as a teacher I described earlier was able to split herself into an authority and a person who has to justify that authority, so when such a pupil is criticized in formal code, they can manage the emotional impact of that criticism by splitting themselves into a pupil who must accept criticism from teachers and a person who can formulate plans to do better. With two codes, there are always two places for you to be, two or more sides to who you are. With only one code, you are trapped, unable to separate yourself from what the world presents you with. While public language is about being connected and formal language is about being separate, together they allow for separability, the formation, dissolution and reformation of relationships with authority.

4　Ulrich Beck
Inequality, risk and separation

Introduction

In Part 1, I argued that in the course of the development of Western society, performances of separateness have become associated with high social status. This development concerns me because, as I suggested in Chapter 1, it has blunted our ability to address questions of children's value with the suppleness of thought and feeling that they require. In societies concerned with high status performances of separateness, children's rights and self-possession are easily seen as an inappropriate bid for separateness, even as a bid for dominant status over adults. In the present section, my task is to illustrate my case, giving reasons to believe that the association between high status and the performance of separateness is a contemporary reality and to argue that contemporary Western societies are fixated on personal separateness. To this end, in the previous chapter, I offered an interpretation of Bernstein's work on social class and linguistic codes (Bernstein 1971). I described the links he drew between high status occupations, relations of authority within schools and a linguistic code – formal code – that maximizes the separateness of its speakers from others. Speaking this code is, in my terms, one way of performing separateness, in this case separateness from other speakers. I also found evidence that Bernstein's sociology was highly sensitive to the performance of separability. His work suggests that the ability to switch between formal and public codes gives middle-class pupils an emotional separability that allows them at least to tolerate, and often to thrive, in the morally complex and emotionally demanding institutional environment of the school. It is important to note that this separability is not officially acknowledged or taught. Schooling demands and celebrates formal code, but it is not the separateness of formal code alone that allows high status middle-class life, with its complex relationship to authority, to proceed. The secret of middle-class life, the secret of feeling at one with authority at large, lies in separability, in the ability to oscillate between separation and connection, formality and informality that is made possible by intimate familiarity with the two-code system.

Hopefully, the illustrations of Bernstein's work I gave in the last chapter resonated with many readers. Many of his observations certainly map onto my own experience of schooling in England from the mid-1970s to the mid-1980s. But, clearly, sociology from the 1950s cannot fully support a case about the distribution of human value and status in *contemporary* society. We may suspect, for example, that many of Bernstein's touchstones, such as social class, and educational and occupational structure, have changed a great deal since the post-war years. So in the present chapter I have chosen to examine the more recent work of the German sociologist Ulrich Beck (1992). Through his commentary on European industrial societies, he gives a valuable overview of major social changes that have taken place in Europe since the mid-twentieth century. He can therefore clarify some of the doubts we might have about using Bernstein to tell us about separateness and separability today. But his value to us is more than ancillary. Beck also has a distinctive view of the relationship between persons, performances of separateness and economic survival that is of great significance for the argument I am developing. It is Beck's contention that although Western societies are still marked by inequalities, the degree to which inequalities are shaped by the social class divisions familiar to Bernstein has been decreasing for decades. Bernstein's typical individuals had a clear sense of who they were, where they were going and what counted as a good person. Their position in society, the opportunities that were likely to arise for them, their expectations and their morality were, for the most part, consequences of their class identity. In Beck's view, social class is no longer such a governing factor. The power of social class to shape our identities and values has decreased as changes in the labour market have rendered class increasingly obsolete as an organizing principle.

In describing Beck's argument I will need to be careful. It is easy to imagine that he is espousing the, clearly inaccurate, view that no-one suffers hardship or inequality any longer. In fact, his view is far more subtle than this and more critical of contemporary society. Many do experience hardship, inequalities are still deep and multiple, but what hardships we face, we increasingly face alone, without class solidarity or class-based value systems to cushion us. We live in a world that increasingly respects only those capable of performing separateness, of living up to its standards of isolation, a world that seems equally razor-toothed whether seen through nostalgia for working-class solidarity or through the vanities of middle-class decency. Through processes of 'individualization' (Beck 1992), class inequality has been transformed into each and every individual's risk of economic annihilation, a risk that is often most effectively countered, I will argue, by performances of separateness. Before I discuss Beck (1992), however, I need to retrace a few steps I have already taken to make sure that I get a firm grip on the roots of his sociological concerns.

Honour and industry

One of the central concerns of nineteenth-century sociology was with how people ever came to think of themselves as individuals. From the perspective of our highly individualistic industrial societies it is sometimes hard to see this as needing explanation. We might, for example, think of ourselves as 'naturally' individual, each of us having a separate body from everyone else and each of us having a mind of our own. This common-sense, naturalistic view may or may not be valid. However, when we further clarify the sociological puzzle presented by the phenomenon of the individual, it becomes clear that the naturalistic view alone cannot explain very much. In Chapter 2, I described Taylor's (Taylor and Gutmann 1992) account of the formation of the individual. The figure of the individual emerged as societies based on the principle of honour were transformed into societies based on the principle of dignity. In the European honour system, persons were valued according to how closely they were connected to a monarch. Apart from the monarch, persons had no value in their own right. Whether or not they were individuals in any 'natural' sense, they were not treated as such, nor were the vast majority under any pressure to act as such – to become distinctive and to mark out their own identity – since their social identity had already been decided by the accident of their birth. The problem for a naturalistic individualism is that, on its own, it cannot explain the existence of institutions, like monarchy and honour, that do not respect it. This is why sociologists of the nineteenth century thought that individualism needed another sort of explanation, one that took into account the possibility that it is certain institutions, or ways of organizing social and economic life, that create and shape individuality, not 'nature' alone.

From the perspective of the politics of identity, Taylor (Taylor and Gutmann 1992) has provided a valuable sketch of the emergence of the individual. He has not, however, provided an account of what factors may have caused honour to decline and dignity to rise. He tells us that the individual emerges along with changes in social institutions, but he does not tell us why those social institutions changed. For such an account, we can turn to Marx (Marx and Engels 1998). On his view, monarchic or feudal society made the monarch the focus and source of all human value, because that person was the focus of all economic value. Aside from trade in luxury goods and the small businesses of craftsmen, economic activity in feudal societies was agricultural, using land as its main raw material. Ownership of land gave economic power. Land could either be inherited or taken by force so there were plenty of opportunities for dispute over ownership. Investing one person – the monarch – with the power to settle disputes and to make ownership legitimate and unarguable, meant greater social stability. The honour system allowed for contention and competition for land and power, but also staved off a descent into unremitting conflict. As long as the majority of economic activity was based on the relatively static raw material of land, connection to the monarch was of paramount importance.

For Marx, European feudalism declined because, over time, new forms of economic activity emerged that were much less reliant on land ownership for the creation of economic value. Feudal lords and peasants were, respectively, experts in possessing and in tending the relatively static raw material of agricultural land. Feudalism had drawn them together in a form of co-operative economic activity. The seeds of change were to be found in the increasing cooperation of traders and craftsmen, respectively experts in transporting and in transforming a wide range of relatively mobile raw materials. This cooperation eventually resulted in the emergence of industrial capitalism, fundamentally changing the economic base of society. As land declined in significance, so did honour.

Industry and liberation

So far, I have offered an explanation of the decline of honour, but how are we to account for the emergence of dignity, the principle of respect for each and every individual regardless of their background? As I have already suggested, the transformation of agricultural societies into predominantly industrial societies was a gradual one. It took place over centuries rather than decades, and affected economic, cultural and political spheres of society at different speeds. This meant that there was time for the industrial or bourgeois classes to develop their own individualistic system of human value, a system that matched their way of creating economic value. Dignity was developed by the bourgeoisie in opposition to the feudal powers they still encountered and negotiated with in their daily affairs. Dignity reflected the new opportunities and prospects that had emerged with industrial society. It reflected a way of creating economic value that was not focused on one monarch, but was distributed among many persons, and that was not based on a single static resource but on the transformation of many resources. Since ownership of land was no longer essential to the generation of wealth, there was no obvious reason why anyone should not make their own choices and their own identity, to transform themselves by gaining and trading on a craft skill, a shipment of goods or an entrepreneurial outlook. In these circumstances, the 'individual' looked like the result of the liberation of society from hundreds of years of feudal oppression. No longer need we be measured by the strength of our connection to other people of higher status; instead, we could be measured by our own actions. In industrial society, we could create ourselves, and to do this we needed the barriers to our freedom of action and association to be removed.

Though the history of dignity is punctuated by the French and American liberal revolutions of the eighteenth century, the dissolution of feudal power was made up of many small, mundane instances of the liberation of action. But while dignity and individualism emerged within specific processes of liberation of action such as the creation of new trading partnerships and new markets, it also gave rise to an abstract and ideal concept of individual freedom, which inspired the slogans of liberal revolution. While specific liberations were always limited to specific persons and groups, the promise of individual freedom was extended to all. This made it possible for people who saw relatively little immediate benefit from any specific liberation nevertheless to count themselves as individuals with dignity, and to interpret their lives, hopes and struggles through the abstract concept of individual freedom. Dignity grew both as the economic base of society changed and as hope for a generalization of liberation took hold of the popular imagination.

Industrialization and class consciousness

Though Marx celebrated the many objective liberations from feudal oppression that were made possible through industrialization, he was highly critical of nineteenth-century industrial society. From his point of view, the problem was that the abstract idea of individual freedom had remained credible long after processes of genuine liberation had stalled. Rather than delivering on its early promise of universal individual freedom, industrialization had produced a new form of inequality. There were some, a minority, who through good fortune, family inheritance or skill and hard work, benefited from industrialization. They came to own factories and to control the flow of raw materials. There were others, a majority, who had no such luck. These different fates interacted with the promise of universal freedom and dignity to produce at least four different patterns of self-understanding or 'consciousness'.

Imagine that the industrial system had benefited you considerably. Imagine that your business decisions and investments had transported you over the years from the position of running a small business, or managing a small inheritance, to that of controlling an industrial empire or a considerable investment fund. Your participation in industry had made you socially mobile and had worked an objective transformation in who and what you were. For such persons, industrial society gave the opportunity of making a fetish of their achievement. They could understand themselves as having achieved simply by living out the promise of freedom, a promise that had been made to all. With this in mind, it was possible to think of oneself as the sole author of one's fate, to admit a little luck, but to emphasize the hurdles one had overcome, the transcendence of obstacles placed in one's path. Such persons could think themselves as embodiments of industry, owing nothing or very little to their background. We have encountered this 'self-made' individual before in Chapter 2.

The robust self-regard of the bourgeois class developed in a context where the accumulation of wealth could be understood as the fulfilment of the promise of individual freedom. Crucially, in this pattern of consciousness, the past was composed of a series of illegitimate or unfortunate restrictions that had been overcome through courage and diligence, rather than a series of advantageous positions made possible by the shape of the industrial economy. For those whom industrialization favoured, personal biography could be tailored to fit the historical narrative of liberation from feudal constraint. This was a story of separation from the past, from ties of belonging and from illegitimate control. This imagination of self was a key performance of separateness. It involved a systematic inattention to dependence on the industrial system as a whole, a system extending to the agencies of the nation-state which provided, among other things, a ready source of cheap labour, an army for quelling social unrest, a navy for defending trade routes and, in many European states, an Empire to guarantee access to raw materials at cheap rates.

Not all industrialists were as vain as I have suggested, nor would many have held consistently to such a self-aggrandizing consciousness. Quite a different understanding of success was widely available through Christian religions. It was possible for successful individuals to understand their position as the result of God's providence, and to think of themselves as doing God's work through industry (Weber 2002). Rather than placing themselves heroically at the centre of their biographies, they could place their God at the centre. Many industrialists of the eighteenth and nineteenth centuries took this view and were thereby inspired to provide good housing for their employees, to campaign against the slave trade that brought so much revenue to the state and against poverty (Nevaskar 1971). On a Marxist view, however, these benefactors had simply replaced the fetish of the self with the mystification of social and economic relations through the terms of faith.

What patterns of consciousness were available to the majority of the population? What of those who were so positioned that they could not significantly alter their circumstances, no matter how hard they worked? In Marx's view, the industrial proletariat were faced with an alternative. They could either endorse the slogans of individual freedom, nursing hopes that their individual liberation would one day emerge from hard work and good fortune, or they could base their consciousness on what they shared with others who were in the same economic position, others of their class. For Marx, the first, aspirational form of consciousness was self-defeating (Marx and Engels 1998). If the majority of the population was exploited, this exploitation was much easier to achieve if the more active and able dreamed that they would be rich one day, separated from their current peers and distinguished from their background. Marx much preferred that the proletariat admit their disadvantaged position and, by respecting each other as equals, turn a potentially shaming class position into a source of pride, a strong collective identity. Collective dignity, a pride in origins and in community became available as a source of value. It gave people practical support by encouraging mutual aid, political power through the establishment of trade unions and political parties, and a sense of identity that could hold a person together in a world of much hardship, frustration and disappointment. As is well known, Marx hoped that the development of this class consciousness would lead to communist revolution throughout the industrialized world, that communism would eventually bring the material benefits of trade and industry to everyone, and that the promise of liberation would be made good in the shape of collective rather than individual freedom.

Performing separateness, performing solidarity

Whatever we might think about Marx's value judgements and predictions (Marx and Engels 1998), his account tells us a good deal about the effects of industrialization on matters of human value. Industry liberated us from feudal inequality between aristocrat and commoner and gave strength to the idea of individual freedom and dignity. But it ended up producing a new form of inequality between the bourgeoisie and the proletariat. Seen against the backdrop of the promise of universal freedom, the actual experience of inequality needed to be accounted for. As people asked themselves where they stood in the industrial world and wondered why, patterns of consciousness emerged which were, to a large extent, distributed on a class basis. High status persons could easily identify themselves with the historical narrative of individual liberation, seeing themselves as separated from the past, and performing as if independent. Low status persons could seek strength and protection through collective identification, acting as members of a community with a shared history and a shared predicament. Arguably it is these distributions of separateness and togetherness that underlie the differences in language use that Bernstein analysed. On this view, the use of public language or restricted code and the rejection of formal language were not the result of linguistic deficiency, but were an accomplishment, an ongoing performance of solidarity. By the mid-twentieth century, then, the performance of separateness was both a means by which class identity could be expressed and a means by which high status could be sought. For those who were stuck with low status, or who willingly accepted it, collective identity, built from the celebration of mutuality and the preservation of community ties, formed a protective cushion against low self-esteem, hardship and frustration and a bulwark against the dominance of the values of the wealthy.

Individualization

So far I have described the twin developments of separateness and solidarity in response to industrialization. By the mid-twentieth century, each ethic had become so embedded in Western European societies that they not only informed individuals' identities, but also gave representative democracy the left–right bipartisan structure so typical of the times. For many, class consciousness had taken on the form of a tradition, with successive generations of working-class people reproducing the union memberships and voting behaviours of their parents and grandparents. Working-class identity was about family, community and friendship. As I suggested above, however, Beck (1992) argues that in the late twentieth century, the conditions that made collective class consciousness a popular response to inequality are no longer in place. The last half of the twentieth century saw the gradual disappearance of alternatives to the ethic of separateness. Beck calls this process 'individualization'. Just as I cautioned above, we should not imagine that Beck is suggesting that inequality has disappeared. Rather, he argues that the socioeconomic landscape has changed so much that traditions of social solidarity are harder to maintain. They are harder to maintain because they rely on activities and attitudes that can, under present circumstances, actually threaten economic well-being. Beck's (1992) arguments cover a wide range of topics including gender relations, the politics of science and technology and the future of the political sphere. I have chosen to concentrate on the changes he charts in the sphere of economic production, the sphere of education and work.

Individualization and the labour market

The spread of education geared toward paper qualifications is a key factor in the process of individualization as Beck (1992) sees it. Education for paper qualifications shapes attitudes, conduct and life chances. In my discussion of the division of labour in Chapter 3, I noted that in complex societies, getting a job tends to require the possession of paper qualifications gained through schooling and examination, rather than personal recommendation alone. From the point of view of the government, a system of paper qualifications, as opposed to a system of personal recommendation, is a useful way to increase the efficiency of the labour market. Employers can selectively recruit staff with a greater degree of confidence, knowing that a well-qualified person has, at least, a track record of carrying out instructions. A widely recognized system of qualifications also broadens prospective employees' choices, liberating them from their immediate social circumstances. Paper qualifications promise to cut wastage of talent on the understanding that a well-informed market is an efficient market. In line with this reasoning, post-war European governments have sought to increase participation in education by raising school-leaving ages, boosting participation rates in post-compulsory education and by expanding the university sector. How have these developments contributed to individualization?

As Beck points out, 'it is only possible to pass through formal education by individually succeeding by way of assignments, examinations and tests' (1992: 94). The very structure of education, then, presents students with records of their individual achievement and demands that each student reflect upon that record. While reflecting on their record it is made clear to students that they should bear in mind that education is a selective process in which performance and future opportunity are closely linked. Schooling thus encourages individual aspiration by explicitly or implicitly setting targets for individual students. Once students aspire, they can begin to make choices and projections about their future. In a labour market based on qualifications, anyone hoping to 'inherit' a job on the basis of family tradition is likely to lose out. Such a labour market prefers those who are willing and able to see their career primarily as their own individual project as opposed to part of a family tradition. As Beck (1992) notes, the individualizing aspects of this form of education apply even in circumstances where students cannot realistically expect to achieve significant upward social mobility through their qualifications. The mind-set required is identical even if a good school, college or university performance only gives protection against downward mobility.

Once qualified, at basic, intermediate or graduate level, and ready to seek work, young people face a further individualizing factor. In a highly differentiated labour market, their local economy may not provide the type of work they have decided to prepare themselves for. Indeed, it may not provide opportunities of any kind. In these circumstances they will be faced with a choice, to remain in the town of their birth or upbringing and suffer potentially harsh economic consequences or to move to another part of the country. There is clearly a tension between the demands of the labour market and ties of family, community and friendship. The experience of having to 'start again' in a new region clearly weakens the commonalities of experience that once made for solidarity. It also makes one's destiny one's own. The expectations and values of the people you grew up with may no longer seem relevant.

Having gained qualifications that mark them out as individuals of some achievement, and having exercised choice over where and how to live and what to aspire to, young people are then exposed to a further individualizing factor. If they find themselves working among similarly qualified colleagues, as is the likely outcome of the contemporary labour market, the qualifications that once marked them out now make them indistinguishable from their colleagues. If they want to be promoted, they must advertise their uniqueness and individual accomplishments. Despite their common background and experience, colleagues are compelled to avoid solidarity and to maximize their performance of separateness. These objective tensions may explain the currency of the mantra 'team player' which demands that employees imagine themselves, often against their better knowledge, to be working in an environment that rewards cooperation. As Beck puts it, 'community is dissolved in the acid bath of competition' (1992: 94). The only way to improve one's circumstances, or even to maintain one's position, is constantly to disavow connection with, similarity to and dependence on others.

Conclusion

I began this chapter by indicating a need to bring my account of separateness up to date and to illustrate how it continues to shape lives, expectations and values in the present day. I believe that Beck's (1992) observations about contemporary individualization demonstrate that the association between performances of separateness and high status has not only persisted into the late twentieth and early twenty-first centuries, but now extends its influence over the majority of the population of Western societies.

In my account so far I have tried to explain why separateness plays such an important role in the distribution of human value. I have also tried to explain why separateness has proved so persistent a factor in the distribution of human value. I have shown that separateness is persistent in its influence because it has been linked over the years to so many of the major economic and political developments that have shaped the contemporary Western world. These developments include the shift from feudal to industrial society, the growth of colonialism and imperialism and the emergence and decline of class society. Given the breadth and depth of the roots of separateness, it is hardly surprising that the association of 'children' with 'rights' is so often interpreted as if it promised actual and complete separation, the generation of monsters and the collapse of love between parent and child.

The aim of this book, however, is not just to describe separateness as a means for the distribution and interpretation of human value, but, more importantly, to give substance to the separability that I found at work in the Convention. The greater the role of separateness in contemporary society, the more it shapes our lives and dominates our judgements, the more effort it will take to show that an alternative approach to human value, such as appears in the Convention, has a history of its own, has substance of its own and is as 'realistic' as separateness. This is the burden of the rest of the book.

PART 3
SEPARABILITY AND INTEGRATION

In Chapter 1, I suggested that for many, the term 'children's rights' raises the spectre of children's actual and complete separation from parents, relatives, community or culture. I suggested that if we take this view to its apocalyptic extreme, children's rights threaten to bring all familiar ways of valuing children, all traditional means by which ideas of human value are passed on, to an end. I then argued that, as they are expressed in the Convention, children's rights are best understood as building on 'separability' rather than separation. Thus, as children's rights are recognized and realized, we should not expect to see greater separation between adults and children, but, instead, a clearer discrimination between happy and abusive relationships. Within a rights-based approach, all the ways that adults and the adult world have of possessing and valuing children could be examined and considered against the backdrop of children's self-possession. For these reasons, it seems clear to me that love and rights, possession and self-possession can co-exist and interact without giving rise to overwhelming conflict between generations. I am not at all convinced, however, that my optimism is widely shared. It feels more natural to many to see children's rights, especially their rights to participate in decision-making, as a threat.

Why might children's rights appear threatening? Some adults might simply want to hold onto whatever power they have, regardless of children's well-being. They would quite correctly recognize children's rights as a threat to their position. Others might find sufficient legitimation for familiar, 'traditional' relationships in the very familiarity of those relationships. For them, critically examining tradition is inherently threatening, even though the likelihood is that such an examination would find much to celebrate and to strengthen. But there is a third, rather more complicated pathway to feeling threatened by children's rights. While the two pathways I have touched on so far involve attachments to illegitimate power or to unquestioned tradition, the third pathway involves a systematic confusion between separateness and separability. I have argued that this systematic confusion saturates thinking about human value in cultures that are based on questioning hierarchies of power and challenging tradition. In these 'modern', Western cultures, separability is systematically confused with actual and complete separation because high status is granted to those able to pass their separability off as separateness. In key cultural performances, many small, partial and temporary instances of separability are mistaken for a fantastic quality of separateness and independence. I will now briefly illustrate this theme with some of the examples I have covered so far. As I proceed, it will be important to remember that these daily performances of high status separateness are not always easy to maintain.

I have given a few illustrations of the performance of separateness in the last few chapters. In each case the performance of separateness is maintained only on the back of many temporary, partial instances of separability. Further, for the performance to be convincing, both to performers and to their audience, this separability must remain obscured and unstated. As I described in Chapter 2, attempts have been made to establish hierarchies of human value on the basis of separation from nature. This performance of separateness may have benefited some nineteenth-century European men, allowing them to look down on non-Europeans, women and children, but if we bear in mind the fact that these men were also biological bodies, their 'separation' from nature could clearly only be partial and temporary, however cultured they were. In Chapter 3, I described Bernstein's (1971) formal code as a use of language that maximizes speakers' distance from their audience, and that had become associated with high status and with middle-class mores and lifestyle. I then suggested, however, that being comfortable with authority and being able to flourish within formal institutions depended on a person's ability to flip between formality and informality, between formal and public codes. Once again, seeing the bigger picture revealed separability invisibly at work in a context that is ostensibly about separateness. Consider the figures I introduced in Chapter 4, Beck's (1992) thoroughly individualized workers. The labour market drives them toward separation, leaving family and old friends behind. Are these workers lonely and unhappy, their separateness as workers mirrored in social isolation? Not all of them are. Once again, separability is key here. Workers' susceptibility to mental illness, substance abuse and addictions will be reduced to the extent that they can comfortably break and reform relationships with the different sets of strangers they meet throughout their career, to the extent, in other words, that they proceed as if separable within, rather than separate from, their immediate social milieu.

In summary, I have argued that those whose lives are shaped by an association between performances of separateness and the achievement of high social status are like mountaineers, each day climbing toward separateness. Like mountaineers, they must not look down. Their performance depends on the temporariness and partiality of separability. But if they acknowledge this, they might lose their nerve. If they lose their nerve, they will fall back into nature, back into the past, back into what they have learned to see as failure and dependency.

These people, often modern, achievement-oriented Westerners are just as likely to misunderstand and to fear children's rights as anyone who is committed to a strongly 'traditional' culture. Their adulthood, defined by their independence, by their ability to perform separateness, depends on their ability to remain unaware of and mistaken about separability, even as they use its resources to generate their status. They mistake the possibility of children's separability for actual and complete separation, because this is what they have become accustomed to do when considering their own identities and place in the world. It is time to restate these ideas in the simplest terms. Children's rights imply comparison between what it is to be an adult and what it is to be a child. Living as a modern Western adult often involves attempts to see oneself as separate from nature, from one's background, from the past, different, in short, from the children we once were. From this perspective, comparisons can only seem threatening, spelling a loss of power, and a collapse into what is understood as a state of actual and complete dependency.

At the end of Chapter 1, I suggested that in order to understand and implement children's rights we need 'flexible' ways of thinking about human value. By now it should be clear that I think this flexibility, which amounts to an easy acquaintance with separability, would not only benefit children, but might directly benefit adults too. The problem is that history has given us ways of valuing ourselves and each other that are brittle, that counterpose independence and dependence, separateness and embeddedness and allow no 'wiggle-room' or exchange between them. This is why love and rights seem so opposed, why possession and self-possession seem incompatible as ways of understanding children's value. History hands us tools of thought made for old tasks. When the task at hand was that of establishing hierarchies of human value, then separateness was a useful tool. It split some of our ancestors off from nature, the past or their backgrounds, setting distance between high and low status persons and groups along a line of development. But if we can now question the sense and value of that task of building hierarchies out of human variety, what a relief it might be to set down the old tools. We might take a new approach, one in which, to value ourselves and each other, we do not need to denigrate nature, the past or the condition of childhood. We can stop pretending that some people are closer to nature, more primitive than ourselves. We can begin again to practise human dignity, this time without regard for chronological age.

I am obviously not alone in wanting equality of respect for children. But many other academic approaches to the issue have been caught up in old struggles, wrangling with the worst of the nineteenth century. As I suggested in Chapter 2, critical developmental psychology seeks equality for children by attempting to discredit the idea of the individual that lies at the heart of Taylor's dignity. I agree that the abstract Western individual is often an unrealistic and profoundly ideological figure, but only when it is founded on a fantasy of actual and complete separation. A model of the individual built out of partial and temporary separabilities might be more acceptable. In the next few chapters, with the particular help of Winnicott (1971) and Deleuze and Guattari (1983, 1988) I will sketch some of the contours of this individual. In a different vein, the sociology of childhood has tried to give children all the opportunities to speak, to be heard and to be taken seriously that dignity requires. It has fought the over-generalized picture of the 'universal child', a creature defined by natural limits and incompetences, instead asserting children's individuality. It has tried to rescue the child from a state of dependency by distancing the child from nature and from the past. This is the value of the mantra 'childhood is socially constructed'. The sociology of childhood thus risks repeating the old fixation on separation.

So far then, we in the late twentieth and early twenty-first centuries have sought solutions to the, sometimes problematic, sometimes dangerous, cultural position of children by attacking our late nineteenth- and early twentieth-century forebears. Developmental thinkers like Freud (1962) and Piaget (1927) have proved useful and surprisingly vulnerable targets. My aim in this book, however, is not just to criticize what has gone before. What I am trying to do is spy out and consolidate new tools of thought. If it seems natural for many to see love and rights in conflict, we can be sure that this sense of the 'natural' is supported by a history of strategies for producing and distributing human value. I want to know what tools of thought, what strategies, will make the peaceful co-existence of love and rights seem natural, something that future generations will take for granted. What words can be used to describe and so to strengthen what, in my view, many people, like parents and children, already live – a non-contradiction between possession and self-possession? To this end I have so far sought out 'separability' at work in a legal document and in some sociological studies. But does it crop up anywhere that is more strategically located for the task of changing what we think of as natural in childhood and natural in relations between adults and children? Fortunately it does. There are a number of mid-twentieth-century authors whose approach to development seems to me to incorporate just the sensitivity to separability that I think we need. So in this section I will examine the work of Carol Gilligan (1982) and D.W. Winnicott (1971). I bring these two together because both have a deep understanding of the tension between separateness and connection and both offer ways to deal with that tension. They are concerned with cultural and personal integration and they both see something like separability as key to that integration.

5 Carol Gilligan
Gender, moral judgement and separability

Introduction

So far in this book I have concentrated on the sociological side of questions of human value. I have asked how and under what conditions value has been ascribed to groups and to individuals. In this chapter I turn to the psychological side of the issue. Human value is not just ascribed to people. People also create value when they decide whether a given course of action is right or wrong. For centuries, philosophers have attempted to discover or to build firm bases for moral judgement. The clear alternative to carrying out this work is to decide that there is no moral value in the world, that all judgements are either arbitrary or are mere reflections of the self-interest of the one who judges. These nihilisms may at some basic level be correct or incorrect. It may be possible or impossible to achieve the firm foundations for moral judgements that hopeful philosophers have worked for. The fact is that most people's everyday moral thinking and feeling take place without much concern for the philosophical poles of certainty and nihilism but are, nevertheless, still highly complex.

In the mid-twentieth century, this complex moral terrain was claimed for the discipline of psychology. Piaget's (1927) theories of child development are, in part, his attempt to claim the philosophical area known as 'epistemology' for psychology, to open questions of 'how we know what we know' to empirical investigation. Lawrence Kohlberg (Colby and Kohlberg 1987) built on Piaget's theories of children's cognitive development to produce a theory of moral development. His work opens questions of 'how we decide what is right and wrong' to empirical investigation. Like Piaget, Kohlberg thought that the best way to study human faculties is to watch them grow, hence his focus on children and development. As I will show, Kohlberg identifies one style of moral reasoning as the most highly developed of them all. In his view, one way of deciding what is right and what is wrong is more advanced than any other. He calls it 'Stage 6' (Colby and Kohlberg 1987: 19) and associates it with autonomy of moral judgement. In order to understand Kohlberg's work (Colby and Kohlberg 1987), it is important to remember that his conclusions concern the *structure* not the *content* of moral reasoning. Though the contents of moral codes may vary from place to place and time to time, the burden of his argument is that a single most highly developed form of moral reasoning is universally available to human beings, even if they do not always reach that level.

Though she studied under Kohlberg, Gilligan (1982) could not accept the universality of a single paramount style of reasoning. As I will show, she had reasons to believe that Kohlberg's work had, at best, charted only half the world of moral experience. In her view, Kohlberg had ignored distinctive styles of moral reasoning that are deployed mainly by women. It is important to note from the outset that Gilligan's (1982) work could not have been conducted without the broadening of knowledge of human value and experience that took place through feminist movements of the twentieth century. I will not, however, be arguing that Gilligan's (1982) vision of morality is superior to Kohlberg's (Colby and Kohlberg 1987) or, to put it simply, that women's morality is better than men's. Drawing on Gilligan's (1982) own writings and one small subsidiary exchange in the ongoing controversy between her and Kohlberg, however, I will illustrate just how important a version of separability is to Gilligan's argument.

Even in these brief introductory comments, you may already have recognized in Kohlberg that same commitment to measuring and establishing the distance between child and adult that I commented on in Chapter 2. In the distinction between content and structure that Kohlberg uses you may also have detected an interest in separateness, this time taking the form of a preference for abstraction. To make my argument in this chapter, I do need to highlight these commitments in Kohlberg's work (Colby and Kohlberg 1987). But it is not my intention to make my own negative judgement of these commitments. Abstraction and autonomy have their value. Indeed, it would be difficult to conceive of such a valuable idea as universal human dignity without them. But as I compare Kohlberg's work (Colby and Kohlberg 1987) and Gilligan's (1982) work, it will become apparent that they differ over the, by now familiar, tension between separation and attachment. Kohlberg sees separation in the form of fully autonomous abstract moral reasoning as the acme of moral development, while Gilligan points out that many women have access to rich and complex moral deliberations that can only be misunderstood when compared to an abstract standard. The tension might be described as one between 'justice' and 'care'. My own concern with 'rights' and 'love' clearly has parallels with it. My next step in this chapter is to describe Kohlberg's stage model of moral development in greater detail. I will begin by outlining the key stages of moral development according to Kohlberg (Colby and Kohlberg 1987). I will discuss how he arrived at his findings, and I will then draw out evidence of his commitment to 'moral autonomy' (Colby and Kohlberg 1987: 19), which is, in my terms, a form of separateness. I will then be in a position to address Gilligan (1982).

Kohlberg's stages of moral development

As with Piaget's (1927) model of general cognitive development, the starting point in Kohlberg's (Colby and Kohlberg 1987) model of moral development is 'egocentrism'. As you will recall from Chapter 2, this 'egocentrism' is not a matter of thinking of oneself as more important than others, but is an inability to recognize the difference between self and other and between one's psychological 'inside' and the 'outside' world. Thus, in the first stage of moral development, individual infants cannot recognize that they are separate from other people or that people may have different interests and viewpoints than their own. In consequence, at stage 1, questions of right and wrong can only be addressed in terms of not breaking rules that are backed up by punishment and not being 'naughty' by causing physical damage to persons or property. What passes for morality at this stage is wholly shaped by infants' egocentrism, by their inability to distinguish between their own perspective and that of the authority figures around them. Thus, a small child at stage 1 will be able to recognize some of their behaviour as 'naughty' in the terms given to them by authority figures. This recognition does not, however, necessarily carry over into consistently 'good' behaviour. To be consistently 'good', a child at stage 1 would need constant monitoring. Acceptance of instructions and definitions does not at this stage add up to a consistent internal moral life. Having no proper understanding of their difference from the rest of the world, stage 1 children cannot be said to have moral cognitions of their own. Just as at stage 1 children have no basis on which to make their own moral conduct consistent, so they also have no reasoned basis on which to challenge the moral edicts of authority figures in their lives.

Growing children reach Kohlberg's (Colby and Kohlberg 1987) stage 2 when they have recognized their fundamental separateness from the world. They are no longer crudely egocentric. They understand that people have different interests and points of view from their own. They are also aware that these interests can come into conflict. They have had experience of their desires and intentions being thwarted by parents or others, have assimilated this experience and have accommodated to it by increasing the complexity of their patterns of thought. Where once they could only think in terms of a single unified world of experience, their working model of the world now involves division and difference. It is at this stage that the first glimmerings of consistency of moral conduct and autonomy of moral judgement can be detected. At stage 2, children's conduct can be consistent with their perceived self-interest. Further, their judgements about right and wrong can differ from those of an authority figure because they now have a basis, however limited, for making judgements of their own. Moral reasoning at stage 2 is markedly individualistic and instrumental. It is right to act according to one's own interests and it is right for others to act according to theirs. Where interests come into conflict, there is little sense in persuading each other to alter those interests, or of making a case for the greater importance of one person's interests over another's. Conflict, when it is resolved, is resolved by an agreement to differ or a deal whereby both interests are met. At stage 2 what is right is not entirely defined by authority, yet children lack the means successfully to resist authority. This is because the only conflict resolution device available to them is an agreement to differ. Unless they are negotiating with a peer, this has little moral force. Many parents, for example, are unlikely to be swayed by it.

Kohlberg places stages 1 and 2 together in what he terms the 'pre-conventional' level of moral development. As I have noted, even stage 2 moral reasoning does not make reference to moral principles or grounds other than those immediately present to the child such as instructions from authority or individual interest. In stages 1 and 2, the child does not recognize 'conventions', moral notions that can be consistently applied across different situations. At stage 3, however, convention becomes all-important in the child's moral thinking. Recall how, in stage 2, conflict among peers could be settled by an agreement to differ. Peers who have resolved conflict by means characteristic of stage 2 are no more or less considerate toward one another than they were before or during the conflict. This is because, at stage 2, conflict resolution takes the form of a benign mutual inconsiderateness. The seeds of 'conventional' morality lie in this symmetry. If we agree to differ because we recognize that we have conflicting interests, even though we do not care for each other's interests, we are at least aware that we are similar to each other. Stage 3 moral reasoning builds on this sense of similarity, converting it into the mutuality of what is often referred to as the 'golden rule' – treat other people as you would like to be treated yourself. This golden rule is very busy at stage 3. It brings an awareness of shared feelings, agreements and mutual expectations to the fore in deciding what is right and what is wrong. Mutuality becomes more important than one's own narrow interests. Significantly, stage 3 marks the point of development at which a young person is sophisticated enough to claim moral superiority over an authority figure. Just as children might give trust, loyalty and respect to their parents, so at this stage they would feel that it is wrong if these are not returned to them. The mutuality that forms the base of stage 3 is not simply symmetrical, however. The idea of 'role' appears and helps adapt it to different circumstances. Children not only offer what they would want in return, but also what they would want were they the other person. In consequence, they will be able to differentiate between the obligations they owe to their relatives, to their friends and to strangers. Stage 3 involves a high degree of 'interpersonal conformity', bids to be a good person in your own eyes and in those of others.

In stage 3, moral reasoning is still 'concrete' in the sense that what matters are the people who are affected by your actions. In stage 4, the concerns of stage 3 are replayed at an abstract level. One sees it as right to fulfil a role to the best of one's ability, not just because other individuals expect it of you and might otherwise think less of you, but, more significantly, because of an awareness that an institution or a system or society as a whole would suffer and be weakened by your failure. Consider a sign that says 'Do not walk on the grass'. At stage 1, the sign is simply irrelevant. At stage 2, the sign can be ignored with no moral qualms if its request clashes with your interests. At stage 3 walking on the grass despite the sign might raise moral qualms (Who owns the grass? Am I harming them? Would I like someone else to abuse my property?). At stage 4, however, a conscience, comfortable with abstraction, would ask what would happen to the grass if everyone ignored the sign. Indeed, this conscience may well take the otherwise trivial example of our sign as a moral instance, asking what would happen to society if everybody broke the rules. At stage 4 the perceived function of morality is to maintain the status quo and moral thinking is dominated by a socially conformist 'conscience'. Stages 3 and 4 comprise Kohlberg's level 2, the 'conventional' level of moral development (Colby and Kohlberg 1987). Stages 5 and 6 comprise the third 'post-conventional' level and it is in these stages that the theme of separation in Kohlberg's (Colby and Kohlberg 1987) work is at its most obvious.

At stage 5, the developing people, perhaps by now teenagers or young adults, have understood that the conventions they grew to respect are not always founded on reason, and that many of them are arbitrary. Given this, it becomes important to be able to recognize which are well founded and should always be respected, and which are 'mere' conventions that can be contravened without moral risk. This opens a space for independent, unconventional thought and action. The powerful conformist voice of stage 4 conscience can be stilled. It is by no means inevitable that the person at stage 5 will appear to be a rebel. Even though the conventional nature of conventions has been recognized, conventions can still be seen as valuable when they promote such goals as fairness and general welfare. At this stage, however, the person may be troubled by conflicts between what they believe is morally right and what counts as legal. Imagine, for example, that the government of their country was involved in a war and had international legal support for that involvement. The knowledge that innocent people suffer in legal wars as well as illegal ones, that law does not make things right, can be troubling.

By stage 5, our developing people have reached the view that existing conventions are not always enough to make the world a moral place. Having reached this position, they are ready to move on to stage 6 that, for Kohlberg (Colby and Kohlberg 1987), is the acme of moral development. In stage 6, a person reaches their moral judgements by applying a set of ethical principles that they themselves have chosen or developed over the years. They use these principles to judge local laws and conventions and, when there is conflict between them, they base their decisions on their principles. Typically these are the universal principles of justice that focus on the rights of the individual. They include a commitment to the universal equality of human beings, and to the moral supremacy of procedures of decision-making that are impartial to issues of ethnicity, gender, sexuality, age, and so on.

Commentary

Kohlberg's model has a good deal of surface plausibility (Colby and Kohlberg 1987). Where else can our ability to see beyond our own narrow self-interest come from, if not from a process of active learning about and adaptation to moral, social situations? Can we not use the model to capture and reflect on sections of our own or others' development? The toddler who quickly learned to call her mother 'naughty'. The conformist child who became a teenage rebel. The adult, weighed down by conscience and duty who was liberated by a new political consciousness. Gilligan (1982), however, provides reasons to question this surface plausibility. But before we turn to her, there are some important points to make about exactly how Kohlberg intends us to interpret his model.

First, Kohlberg's stages represent a one-way street of development. Once an individual has moved from, say, stage 2 to stage 3, there is no going back. Movement between stages is not brought about by a person learning moral lessons that they can subsequently forget. Instead, in Kohlberg's view, each person is like a self-programming, problem-solving moral computer. Development happens because individuals take on experience like that of parental authority or arguing with peers, and try to make sense of that experience, thereby changing the way their minds process further information. For example, once people have developed the concept of 'mutuality', they search for mutuality wherever they look, and they grasp and interpret their experiences through this concept. By stage 3, mutuality is part of what they have become. They can no more drop the concept than they can shrink themselves down to fit their baby-clothes. Second, Kohlberg is proposing that his model reflects propensities for moral development that are universal among human beings. If people enjoy all the conditions in which they can develop morally, then they will pass through stages 1 to 6. But there are plenty of people whose moral development has been 'stunted'. If some have got stuck at stage 2, focused solely on pursuing their own interests, and others at stage 4, mistaking rigid adherence to rules for moral adequacy, Kohlberg has given us a way of recognizing them. But, if opportunities to change keep presenting themselves, then stage 6 is the inevitable result of human moral development. This is a bold conjecture indeed, especially given that it is hard to distinguish stage 6 from the commitments of a specifically Western tradition of liberal political and moral philosophy. Kohlberg embraces this comparison and believes it strengthens his model's credibility. Others, who are critical of the liberal tradition – Marxist and other left-wing thinkers, supporters of non-Western cultural and moral traditions – might see this as a reason to distrust his model as too prescriptive, culturally imperialist, or as plain ignorant. Having examined the model, the boldness of Kohlberg's claims and the position of some of his detractors, I will now draw out what I see as Kohlberg's commitment to separateness.

Kohlberg and separateness

Like Piaget (1927), Kohlberg takes the view that we are not born with an awareness of our separateness from the world and that we must produce this knowledge for ourselves by assimilating and mentally accommodating ourselves to early experience. Without the separation between self and world that brings egocentrism to an end, no further development can take place. Like Piaget, Kohlberg also sees development as a series of elaborations of this knowledge of separateness. To move from stage 2 to stage 3 it is necessary to separate oneself from one's own, narrow self-interest. Moving from stage 3 to stage 4 involves a separation from a direct concern with other concrete individuals and a refocusing of moral concern on an abstraction like a group, an institution or a society. The transition from stage 4 to stage 5 is one from a condition of close attachment to conventions, to a relative detachment from them, the stage 5 individual being able to stand outside familiar values and rules and, from that relatively independent vantage point, compare them with alternatives. At stage 6, the moral person is as independent as it is possible to be, choosing and developing their own ethical position and using that to measure the morality of their own society and its laws. When they find it necessary, a stage 6 person will take a stand against their society and its laws. In short, the acme of Kohlberg's (Colby and Kohlberg 1987) moral development is a self-made, self-regulating individual. At each stage up to stage 6, the developing moral persons separate themselves from something only to re-attach themselves to something more abstract or general. This re-attachment to instrumentality, the golden rule, roles and rules reveals their relative lack of development. The only things to attach to at stage 6 are ethical principles that are already one's own. Attachment in this case is to oneself. It is clear, then, that Kohlberg's model of moral development embodies a straightforward commitment to separation as the measure of moral worth. It hierarchically arranges a variety of moral standpoints, placing the least 'separated' at the bottom and the most 'separated' at the top. The stages are connected by a line of development along which human value is, at least implicitly, distributed. But how did Kohlberg (Colby and Kohlberg 1987) arrive at this model?

Kohlberg's method

Kohlberg's (1976) research was simple and subtle. He conducted interviews on moral topics with people at a range of chronological ages. These interviews were structured so as to provide opportunities to expose the reasoning that lay behind their responses. Typically, Kohlberg would initially present interviewees with a moral dilemma, a short story in which a character has to choose between two courses of action, each of which will break one moral code or another. The interviewee was then asked to say what the character should do and why they should do it. This was followed by a number of probe questions that encouraged the interviewee to explore the dilemma at greater length. Having gathered many interviews like this, Kohlberg's job became one of interpretation. Taking the precise way in which interviewees resolved the moral dilemma and arrived at a moral judgement as his starting point, Kohlberg would work 'backwards', asking himself to imagine what kind of picture of the moral world a person would have, given their means of resolution. Repeated many times, this process of reconstructing individuals' ways of constructing the moral world, gave him a range of moral approaches. Loose correlations between each of these approaches and the chronological age of interviewees, coupled with a sense that some approaches were more complex than others gave Kohlberg the basis on which to arrange them as stages in a line of development.

Now that I have described Kohlberg's stage theory, and shown that it is committed to treating various forms of separateness as the universal measure of moral development, we are ready to move on to consider Gilligan (1982). As I will illustrate over the next few sections, Gilligan's (1982) research led her to believe that Kohlberg's (Colby and Kohlberg 1987) universal stages did not represent a universal human truth but a partial and peculiarly 'Western tradition' (Gilligan 1988: 3) in which the only good and proper selves are those that appear to be separate from others.

Gilligan, girls and moral dilemmas

I will begin my discussion of Gilligan's (1982) work by examining some of her empirical findings. Following Kohlberg (1976), Gilligan decided to examine the cognitive bases of moral judgement by presenting interviewees with dilemmas and asking them how they might be resolved. She was particularly interested in exploring differences in the performance of boys and girls and men and women in these tasks. Here is one of the moral dilemmas that both Kohlberg (Colby and Kohlberg 1987) and Gilligan (1982) used. It is often referred to as Heinz's dilemma.

> In Europe, a woman was near death from a special kind of cancer. There was one drug that the doctors thought might save her. It was a form of radium that a druggist in the same town had recently discovered. The drug was expensive to make, but the druggist was charging ten times what the drug cost him to make. He paid $400 for the radium and charged $4000 for a small dose of the drug. The sick woman's husband, Heinz, went to everyone he knew to borrow the money and tried every legal means, but he could only get together about $2000, which is half of what it cost. He told the druggist that his wife was dying, and asked him to sell it cheaper or let him pay later. But the druggist said, 'No, I discovered the drug and I'm going to make money from it.' So having tried every legal means, Heinz gets desperate and considers breaking into the man's store to steal the drug for his wife.
>
> (Colby and Kohlberg 1987: 230)

The dilemma here is that Heinz's alternative courses of action are both wrong in conventional terms. He can either steal or allow his wife to die. Should Heinz steal the drug?

Gilligan (1982) considers and compares the responses of two 11-year-old children, Amy and Jake, at some length. Jake resolved the dilemma quickly. For him it was simply a question of whether preservation of life or respecting property rights is the more important principle. He addressed the dilemma by establishing a hierarchy between these abstract principles. Heinz should steal the drug because it is a less bad course of action than letting his wife die. Jake also compared moral decisions to mathematics, saying that the moral dilemma is 'sort of like a math problem with humans' (Gilligan 1982: 26). Once his principled decision was made, the resolution of the dilemma was nothing more than logic. Gilligan quotes him as follows: 'For one thing, a human life is worth more than money, and if the druggist only makes $1000 he is still going to live, but if Heinz doesn't steal the drug, his wife is going to die' (Gilligan 1982: 26). Jake then pointed out that money can always be replaced with more money, while individual people like Heinz's wife cannot be replaced at all. For Jake, stealing the drug was the least worst option because it is a wrong that can be made right. The death of Heinz's wife cannot be made right. Jake displayed a good deal of moral sophistication in his answer. When reminded that stealing is against the law, he replied that 'laws have mistakes, and you can't go writing up a law for everything that you can imagine' (Gilligan 1982: 26).

When Gilligan used Kohlberg's (1976) standardized methods to estimate Jake's level of moral development, she found that, overall, his responses were a mixture of stages 3 and 4, but there was also evidence that he reached stage 6 at times. In Kohlberg's (Colby and Kohlberg 1987) terms then, Jake was well on the way to full moral development, to a high capacity for formal thought that would free him 'from dependence on authority and allow him to find solutions to problems by himself' (Gilligan 1982: 27). So, did Amy, another bright and articulate 11-year-old, perform equally well? Asked if Heinz should steal the drug, she replied: 'Well, I don't think so. I think there might be other ways besides stealing it, like if he could borrow the money or make a loan or something, but he really shouldn't steal the drug – but his wife shouldn't die either' (Gilligan 1982: 28). At this point, Amy didn't seem to have engaged with the dilemma at all. As Gilligan writes, she 'seems evasive or unsure' (1982: 28). When Amy was asked why Heinz should not steal the drug, she replied:

> If he stole the drug, he might save his wife then, but if he did, he might have to go to jail, and then his wife might get sicker again, and he couldn't get more of the drug, and it might not be good. So, they should really just talk it out and find some other way to make the money.
>
> (Gilligan 1982: 28)

Once again, Amy seemed to avoid rather than address the dilemma. She applied none of the abstract, principled thinking that Jake used to get a firm grip on the problem. Instead, she concerned herself with the possible implications of Heinz's action for his relationship with his dying wife and displayed a degree of faith that, by communicating, the two would together find a way out of their predicament. Where Jake saw a mathematical problem with people in it, Amy saw an ongoing, developing story of two people's relationship. In her view, Heinz should avoid any course of action that might lead him to being separated from his wife.

When Gilligan (1982) passed Amy's responses through Kohlberg's (Colby and Kohlberg 1987) standardized assessment procedure, Amy scored between stages 2 and 3. As Gilligan writes:

> her responses seem to reveal a feeling of powerlessness in the world, an inability to think systematically about the concepts of morality or law, a reluctance to challenge authority or to examine the logic of received moral truths ... her reliance on relationships seems to reveal a continuing dependence and vulnerability.
>
> (1982: 30)

So far, then, it seems clear that Amy is less developed than Jake. However, by setting Jake and Amy's responses in direct contrast with one another, Gilligan is asking us to think about one, key question: Is Amy, in reality, morally immature or does Kohlberg's (Colby and Kohlberg 1987) scheme have inbuilt limitations that prevent it from hearing her properly? Gilligan guides our thinking on this matter by giving us further examples from her study. Her interviewees, Jeffrey and Karen, were both 8 years old. When they were asked about how they deal with situations in which they are not sure what to do their replies differed, just as Jake and Amy's did.

> *Jeffrey* – When I really want to go to my friends and my mother is cleaning the cellar, I think about my friends, and then I think about my mother, and then I think about the right thing to do. (*But how do you know it's the right thing to do?*) Because some things go before other things.
>
> (Gilligan 1982: 33)

So Jeffrey reported making his decisions by placing needs and persons in a hierarchy or a prioritized 'to do' list. This would enable him to make his decision and have done with the matter, to reduce the complexity of the choice and his degree of involvement with it to a minimum. His approach allows him to solve dilemmas and leave them behind him so that he can carry on with his own activities. How does Karen talk about a similar situation?

> *Karen* – I have a lot of friends, and I can't always play with all of them, so everybody's going to have to take a turn, because they are all my friends. But like if someone's all alone, I'll play with them. (*What kinds of things do you think about when you are trying to make that decision?*) Um, someone all alone, loneliness.
>
> (Gilligan 1982: 33)

Once again, there is a very clear contrast between the response a boy gave and the response a girl gave. At first sight, when compared to Jeffrey, Karen seems to be unable to prioritize. She seems deficient. However, if we pay closer attention, we see that issues arise for Karen that Jeffrey did not consider. Karen did not use moral thinking to pull herself out of the situation to make clear and permanent decisions about it. Instead, she considered herself and her moral choices through the relationships that she had with others. As she thinks about choices, she does not convert her friends into a hierarchy of priorities. To her mind they remain her friends and each is to have a 'turn' playing with her. The moral task, as she sees it, is to make sure nobody is left out. It begins to look as if there is a distinctive moral voice at work here, one that Kohlberg's (Colby and Kohlberg 1987) scheme cannot prepare us to hear.

This moral voice is not about maintaining separation and being in the right, but about maintaining involvement and caring. The contrast is one between justice and care.

As Gilligan (1982) adds more examples of contrasts like this, it becomes apparent that Jake and Amy, Karen and Jeffrey are not unusual cases and that there are grounds for thinking that, somehow, there is a tendency for gender to make a difference to moral thinking. Once again this raises a question. Is it more likely that women and girls are, in reality, less morally developed than men and boys, or is it more likely that Kohlberg's (Colby and Kohlberg 1987) 'universal' scheme is in fact rather limited? Is it possible that Kohlberg's scheme, based on the high value of separateness, is insensitive to or biased against the kind of moral thinking and values that girls and women tend to use? This is indeed one of the conclusions Gilligan (1982) reaches.

Gilligan, morality and the Western tradition

Gilligan does not rely on interview data alone to make her case, though her data say quite a lot. Drawing on her interpretation of centuries of moral thinking in the West, she broadens her argument to consider why Kohlberg was unaware of women's moral 'different voice', the voice of involvement and care. For Gilligan, the Western tradition of moral thinking, of trying to define what it is to be a good person, has, since antiquity, seen men as normal and women as secondary and deviant. In the Old Testament, a woman, made from part of a man (and as something of an afterthought), fails to follow God's rules, with infamous consequences. The Roman epic poet Virgil celebrates the hero Aeneas for his ability to sever attachments to reach his goals. This masculine slant on the question of the good self was repeated throughout the twentieth century. For example, it was clear to Freud how boys gain a sense of morality. They experience separation from their mothers. They envy, even hate their fathers, suspect them of taking their mother away and, fearing paternal retribution in the form of literal or symbolic castration, they resolve their emotional ambivalence toward him by trying to become like father, ultimately respecting and upholding impersonal justice. Women's development was something of a mystery to Freud. Since they did not seem to 'detach' from their mothers like boys, it was easier for him to think of women having 'less of a sense of justice than men' (Freud 1961: 257–8) than to think of women having a different sense of morality. Time and again, according to Gilligan (1982), men's morality has been mistaken for the only, universal morality and women have been measured against this standard and found wanting. Kohlberg was just the latest inheritor of this time-honored prejudice. The task Gilligan chose for herself, however, went beyond criticizing male power and prejudice. Instead she identified a positive project of mapping those spaces of human moral experience that have long been overlooked because of their association with women.

The 'different voice'

To build her picture of the morality of care, instead of presenting hypothetical scenarios like Heinz's dilemma, Gilligan (1982) conducted interviews with women who were facing the real-life decision of whether or not to have an abortion. Here, Anne, a woman in her late twenties, is considering whether or not she should have a third abortion:

> I think you have to think about the people who are involved, including yourself. You have responsibilities to yourself. And to make a right – whatever that is – decision in this depends on your knowledge and awareness of the responsibilities that you have and whether you can survive with a child and what it will do to your relationship with the father or how it will affect him emotionally.
>
> (Gilligan 1982: 78)

A lot of public, political debate about abortion takes place in vocabulary that makes the choices seem clear. Once a 'right to life' is posited, a 'right to choose' is asserted in reply. The debate first turns on the issue of whether either right exists and then on which right is the most important. The tone of Anne's comments is refreshingly different from this. Though she is trying to make a decision, she doubts that it could ever be 'right'. From Kohlberg's (Colby and Kohlberg 1987) perspective, as I have described it, this is just a failure to grapple with the morality of the issue. But if we think again, we can see it as a distinctly productive uncertainty. For anyone who cannot predict the future, being uncertain about being 'right', but still trying to do the right thing, seems a rather balanced position. Once the goal of certainty, of showing oneself and others that one is 'in the right', has been lost, a host of other considerations come into focus. Anne thinks of herself as attempting to balance responsibilities to herself and to others. To do this, she needs first to understand her responsibilities, which means thinking very carefully about her relationships and about the persons in those relationships. If she has a child, will her relationship with the father continue? How will he feel about becoming a father? So much is unknown, and there are so many factors involved, that she can never be certain. Her way of exploring what is reasonable to do reveals a number of things about her basic moral stance. She sees herself as embedded within a network of relationships that are connected by her empathy and compassion. She defines her responsibilities within this network. To think morally does not involve her transcending the network, but involves using it and her knowledge about it to chart a tentative course through uncertainty. Never leaving a network of responsibilities, she is never done with making moral choices. In dealing with her dilemma, Anne does not use abstract principles to simplify it so that she can get away from it quickly. Instead, she recognizes the complexity of the situation and plans to stay close to that complexity, using her insight to monitor its development. She does not so much make a judgement as stay 'in touch'. This may well involve talking to significant people in her life and asking them how they feel and what they want. In these ways, Anne's comments are a good illustration of the morality of care.

Justice, care and separability

It should be clear by now that, in the terms Kohlberg (Colby and Kohlberg 1987) and Gilligan (1982) use, justice is founded on separateness, while care is founded on connection. Justice cannot move without using principles to distance itself from complexity. Care has little meaning outside its networks of responsibility. But how are these moralities to be related to each other? There are at least four possibilities to consider. As I explore them it should become clear that the fourth possibility, Gilligan's own view, involves the phenomenon that I have called 'separability'.

First, we should consider the possibility that Gilligan is simply mistaken and that she has over-interpreted her data. What she sees as a distinct moral orientation of care is, in fact, simply one of the factors in Kohlberg's scheme. Kohlberg himself takes this view:

> In discussing the moral domain Gilligan (1982) not only has postulated sex differences in moral judgement but has made an ideal–typical distinction between a 'care and response orientation' and a 'justice orientation' and claims that our moral stages only capture development of the justice orientation ... it may be noted that many or most moral concerns of care are concerns about enhancing the welfare of other persons or not hurting them and about preserving and embracing relationships with others. We consider the concerns as falling within the domain of justice as the orientations of social utilitarian concern for the welfare of others or the perfectionist orientation of promoting harmonious social relations, Plato's conception of justice.
>
> (Colby and Kohlberg 1987: 24)

Here Kohlberg reasserts the universality not only of his scheme, but, referring to the ancient philosopher Plato, of the Western moral tradition as a whole. If

Kohlberg is correct, justice would remain superior to care, embodying it and having the capacity to speak on its behalf. In response, Gilligan (Gilligan et al. 1988) has assembled further empirical evidence to support her view that justice and care are distinct ways of seeing, hearing and interpreting the moral world. As with many controversies that lie in the overlap of science and morality, there is no end to this exchange of evidence in sight.

The next possibility is that justice and care are in competition with one another, that they are opposites in conflict. As I have argued, care, in practice, is complex and involved. It requires communication and conversation, and it can differ with itself. Care is not the vocabulary of command, control and rapid decision-making. Justice, however, is more fleet of foot. Once the highest principles are found, all subsequent actions can follow without doubt and without hesitation. Further, justice can always justify itself, where care can only say that it tried to do its best. Given these differences, it would hardly be surprising if justice usually won the contest. There is a view that the dominance of justice over care is just one facet of men's historical domination of women. If we examine today's world, the world that is the fruit of the morality of justice, we might well find reason to prefer care and to assert its superiority. Would more justice really make the world a better place, when horrific wars are conducted within its terms and dramatic environmental degradation is permitted on the grounds of the primacy of human life? Noddings (1984) and Ruddick (1989) have both argued that giving power to the care orientation would result in a better world.

A third way of envisioning the relationship between justice and care would result from a rather simplistic mis-reading of Gilligan's (1982) work. If men do justice and women do care, then, as long as everyone stays in their place, all will be well. Justice suits men for a world of public affairs and tough, fast decision-making, and care suits women for caring roles, where there is plenty of time for communication. Vive la différence! But Gilligan (1982) gives us good reasons to question this static picture of the distribution of justice and care between men and women. She writes;

> Attachment and separation anchor the cycle of human life, describing the biology of human reproduction and the psychology of human development. The concepts of attachment and separation that depict the nature and sequence of infant development appear in adolescence as identity and intimacy and then in adulthood as love and work.
>
> (1982: 151)

The way Gilligan has it, justice and care are not in opposition, nor are they arranged as a static pair of gendered book-ends. Rather, each person, regardless of gender, has to deal throughout their life with the promise and the perils of both separateness and connection. Neither justice nor care is 'better' or more important just as neither a child's attachment to or separation from its parents is 'better'. Humans all have to deal with the fact that we need both. She imagines the complementary pair of moral orientations, justice and care, developing out of 'this reiterative counterpoint in human experience' (1982: 151). Throughout our lives we move into and out of moments of separation and individual autonomy and moments of togetherness and mutual dependency. In her view, the association of justice with men and care with women is by no means necessary or inevitable. These associations arise because men and women are usually presented with different paths through the crossing and re-crossing of attachment and separation. This disposes them to try to solve the problems of relating to the world in ways that give emphasis to different aspects of what is fundamentally the same human experience. Neither justice nor care alone can provide a total solution, however. Thus, men and women are often given to distinctive fears about their lives, fears that their way of managing the recurrent tension of attachment and separation is, at some point, going to fail. Typically, men fear loneliness and isolation, while women fear that their identities will be engulfed in the connections they have with others, especially men.

It is my view that the phenomenon of separability can be discerned in this fourth picture of the relationship between justice and care. Neither the terms of justice nor care can fully capture human experience, since that experience is one of partial and temporary separations and re-connections. If we commit ourselves to justice over care or care over justice, we will fail to understand the full implications of the moral choices we make in our lives. If we allow ourselves to be mastered by one orientation to such an extent that it obscures the other from us, we will become confused and vulnerable to self-generated fears. Even though our lives as men and women are still patterned so as to lead us either to justice or to care, Gilligan (1982) shows us that it is both possible and desirable to move between these voices. Let me illustrate this by returning to the apparent conflict between love and rights discussed in Chapter 1. In the topic of children's rights we find a peculiarly tight knot composed of both the attachments and the separations that Gilligan sees as fundamentals of human life. If we approach the issue from the moral standpoint of justice, we may project a fear onto the issue, a fear that justice alone cannot assuage. Our opinions may be driven by the fear that a child alone should not be exposed to the isolation that always haunts independence. If we approach the issue from the moral standpoint of care, we may project another kind of fear onto the issue. We may fear that even when a child is loved, it can be so immersed in relationships that it loses its identity and becomes open to exploitation. Whether we commit to justice or care, if we commit solely to either, we can no longer see the possibility of peaceful co-existence between love and rights in children's lives. It is only by appreciating both moral voices that we can imagine love and rights co-existing peacefully.

Conclusion

In this chapter I have shown that Gilligan (1982) was strategically positioned to detect an association between separateness and high status in Kohlberg's (Colby and Kohlberg 1987) theory of moral development. Her work demonstrated that it is not necessary for a psychologist of moral development to make that association. She also argued that to build this association into a moral theory as if it were a universal and inevitable feature of human life may be a mistake. Gilligan's close attention to the specificity of some women's style of moral deliberation showed that there could be an alternative to the morality of abstraction and separation. The 'different voice' worked through connection, involvement and care. One question remains outstanding, however. If moral development through the justice pathway is about becoming increasingly separated, what might count as moral development along the care pathway? Gilligan (1982) does not pay much attention to this question. Given the nature of care, this is not surprising. With justice, there is always somewhere else to go. Developing out of a 'stage' always means a person 'leaving' their immediate environment. With care, there is no 'leaving', no external position that would give greater advantage, no 'outside' that would even make sense. Perhaps if 'development' is the right word for change that is not marked by increasing distance, then the development of care might be composed of increasingly sophisticated ways of being involved.

Once she had heard the different moral voice, was able to speak it publicly and made it the centre of her working life, Gilligan (1982) did not set about asserting its superiority over justice. This despite the fact that Kohlberg had no qualms about re-asserting the primary status and superiority of the moral voice he studied. To try to reverse the hierarchy would have been true only to a particular ideological version of the moral world, one that equated the dominance of justice with male dominance over women, and equated those two forms of dominance with inequality and violence. Gilligan had another truth to answer to, the experiences, shared across genders, of attachment and separation and the common knowledge that both have their pleasures and fears. Though we live in a world where separation is celebrated and attachment to the personal and historical past and to the 'natural world' is often denigrated, for Gilligan (1982), good sense and maturity lie in not being fixated on either. Though we cannot see the world through justice and through care simultaneously, if we can acknowledge the virtues and limitations of both, we will be more at home with ourselves, less confused by the partial nature of both separations and attachments. It is my view that our condition as humans is one of separability and that if this is made clear, it will be much easier for children to gain equality of respect among all other humans.

In Gilligan's (1982) work, I have found an approach to the psychology of human value that can comprehend both genuine differences in moral viewpoint between people and changes within individuals over time and across situations. What appeals to me most about her work is that though she clearly disowns the hierarchical obsessions around human value that come to us from the late nineteenth and early twentieth centuries, she does not discard justice, rights and the individual, but helps us to broaden what these words might mean to us. As I have previously suggested, one way to help children's rights become a reality is to make separability seem as commonsensical an idea, as 'natural' a feature of human life, as separation is today. By warning us against allowing either justice or care to master us, our values and our moral feelings, Gilligan has made a great contribution.

6   D.W. Winnicott
Insides, outsides and separability

Introduction

In the previous chapter I presented Gilligan's (1982) work as an example of how an easy familiarity with separability can affect what we make of separation and connection, rights and love, self-possession and possession by others. Gilligan built a relationship for herself with ideas of justice and care that was not 'either/or', but was 'both/and'. She did not try to assert care over justice, but refused to champion either one, appreciating that attachment and separation both have their places and times in human lives. Arguably, Gilligan was able to build this relationship because she was looking at the issues from a standpoint that included the experience of having been a child and the experience of raising children. It seems that being a woman and being informed by feminist politics helped Gilligan fully to value this standpoint. Though she was working within and around traditions of enquiry that owe much to Piaget (1927), Gilligan's sense of human value was not based on the transcendence of childhood, of nature and of one's immediate environment, but on recalling the past and knowing that issues of attachment and separation never go away. Gilligan thus put her readers in a position to identify and to appreciate forms of human value, experiences and ways of living that have little to do with the isolated, 'self-made' individual that is more normally celebrated in modern Western societies.

Gilligan was concerned both to consolidate her own views and to counter a powerful tradition of thinking about morality. All this in the context of the politicization of gender. She had her own agenda that clearly cannot be reduced to mine. Nevertheless, I found her helpful in illustrating some aspects of what I have called separability. Gilligan (1982) told us that separation and attachment are both lived within each human life. At times she seems to see them taking place at distinct moments in people's lives. At other times she gives us powerful insights into how 'separated' men and 'attached' women yearn for ways of living that would give them either the intimacy of attachment or the freedom of separation. She also uses the metaphor of 'counterpoint' (1982: 151) to describe the relation between separation and attachment. This metaphor refers to music, like that of the composer Bach, in which two (or more) tunes are played simultaneously to generate a very stimulating tension (Hofstadter 1999). Each of these three aspects of moral life that Gilligan has in mind can be related to the term 'separability' in that each is based on the possibility of moving between conditions of separation and attachment.

Gilligan (1982) has certainly helped me to explore the ways that separability phenomena are distributed over the human life-course and between social groups like men and women. Yet her basic sense of the relationship between separation and attachment is that they are always in tension, always somewhat estranged from one another. This presents me with a difficulty. From an early point in this book, I have relied on terms that imply something rather different about separability phenomena. I have certainly talked about separation being a temporary condition and this chimes in with Gilligan's (1982) thinking. But I have also countered the notion of actual and complete separation with phrases like 'partial separation' and 'partial attachment'. Without denying the manifestation of separability through the life-course and between genders, and without denying that this often takes the form of a tense relationship between separation and attachment, I have relied on an intuition that separability can also involve a 'spatial' overlap of separation and attachment. Let me go through this step by step.

If it makes sense to talk about partial separation, and I think it does, then this must involve partial attachment. If these two 'partials' exist at the same time for the same person, then they must, in some sense, overlap. In concrete terms, this could imply at least two different conditions. First, it could imply that a person can be separated from some aspects of their environment, while being firmly attached to others. Many social gatherings depend on this se-lectivity of attention and attachment. Indeed, it is hard to imagine a social gathering in which everyone is equally involved with every other person in the room at the same time. This first separability phenomenon is little more than common sense. Second, however, an overlap of separation and attach-ment might imply that a given person can be partially separated from and partially attached to their whole environment simultaneously. This second manifestation of separability, subtly different to that examined by Gilligan, need not involve the estrangement of separation and attachment and need not be experienced as a tension. If this line of reasoning makes sense, then it would imply that separability can be manifested through the tense es-trangement of separation and attachment *and* through a complex entangle-ment of the two *and* through their peaceful co-existence.

You may have found my reasoning here rather too abstract and complex to make immediate sense to you. Alternatively, you may have followed my reasoning with confidence but felt that it simply did not make sense. After all, how can something, in this case, separability, be manifested sometimes as 'tension' and sometimes as 'peace', the opposite of tension? Surely this breaks the fundamental rule of logic, the 'excluded middle', which states that something cannot be itself and be its opposite?

This chapter's discussion of the work of the psychotherapist D.W. Winnicott (1971) will take the complex and abstract issues of overlaps between separation and attachment and open them up with his ideas and examples. Winnicott wrote in a very accessible way and this will help me make my concerns more directly relevant to you. If you followed my reasoning, but think it nonsense because a thing cannot be the same as its opposite, Winnicott (1971) will help me be clearer here as well. As I re-interpret his ideas for my purpose of fleshing out the notion of separability, it will become clear that separability is not a 'thing' so does not suffer the limitations that logic places on 'things'. Not only is separability not to be understood as a thing, but through Winnicott (1971), we will see that it is also not a 'relationship'; rather, separability is the possibility of relationship.

I am aware that all this logic and non-logic, all my intuitions and pedantic insistence that separability is 'not this and not that' is hardly appetizing for most readers. So let me finish this introduction with one of Winnicott's (1971) observations that involves the overlap of separation and attachment. What does a piece of string do when it is tied between two objects? It certainly attaches them, one to the other. But it also takes up space between them, so it separates them too.

When the baby cries, she really means it

Winnicott (1971) was one of a group of British psychoanalysts and psychotherapists who, through the middle years of the twentieth century, both built on and differed with Freud's (1962, 1963) psychoanalytic teachings and practice. Their approach is often referred to as 'object relations'. This term reflects their shared interest in factors that affect what individuals make of the various psychologically relevant 'objects' that make up their social milieu. Object relations approaches try to identify and describe healthy and unhealthy ways of relating to the world and then try to account for these patterns in terms of attachment and separation difficulties that are taken to be typical of infancy.

Melanie Klein (1975a, 1975b) was, perhaps, the most prominent figure in object relations. She became a figurehead in a long-running dispute about psychoanalytic theory with Anna Freud, the daughter of Sigmund. I have already commented on the attention that Sigmund Freud gave to biology and to human evolution (see Chapter 2). For him, psychoanalysis was a science, rooted in biological fact. In contrast, Klein's (1975a, 1975b) approach was rooted in an empathic understanding of the ways her clients experienced the world and themselves in relation to the world. She focused on the interpretative work we do 'inside' our own heads to deal with distressing events taking place 'outside'. In this section I will spend some time describing her theories of psychological health and illness. I will then note some important contrasts between her ideas and Winnicott's (1971) work. A discussion of these contrasts should help me to clarify Winnicott's (1971) work and its relation to my term 'separability'.

Imagine that you are three weeks old. You are small, so you feel the cold quite quickly. You are growing, so you are often hungry. You have not yet learned control over your sphincter muscles, so you are doubly incontinent and liable to 'lose your lunch'. You are, in short, extremely vulnerable. There is a warm presence that feeds you and cleans you up. But this presence sometimes goes away. When it is absent, you have no idea when, or even if, it is going to come back. How do we ever survive this level of uncertainty and anxiety?

In Klein's (1975b) view, our survival strategy in the first few months of life is to make sense of the chaos by simplifying it as much as we can. We impose order on our experience by dividing it sharply into 'good' and 'bad'. Objectively speaking, of course, most aspects of the world are completely neutral. They are neither good nor bad in themselves and have no benign or malign intent toward us. In reality, the greater part of the world is oblivious of and indifferent to each of us. But when we are very young, getting an accurate picture of the world and of our place in it has a very low priority. We insist that things are either good or bad, benign or malign, and we persist in applying these judgements as a way of managing our anxieties. Once we have formulated this simplest of responses to anxiety, it remains available to us throughout our lives. Think back to the last bad day you had. At breakfast you dropped and broke a cereal bowl. On the way to work you noticed that the small crack in the windscreen of your car has suddenly got much longer. You forgot which room had been scheduled for the nine o'clock meeting that day, and a change in circumstances meant that you had to do some of last week's work over again. Only four bad things happened, yet, when you tell your friends about it, the whole day stank. You may have felt that, for that day, the world had turned against you. Klein calls this the 'paranoid-schizoid position' (Klein 1975b).

Returning to infancy, this stark splitting of the world into good and bad, and the rejection of the possibility that anything is neutral, gives us our first chance to see the world as a positive and hospitable place for us rather than as a chaos. Splitting lets us start to trust and to love. When our carer, who Klein (1975b) identifies as 'mother', is with us, looking after us, we project absolute undiluted goodness onto her. She is a 'good object'. When she absents herself, however, we project absolute undiluted badness onto her. She may have been called away from us, innocently, to answer the telephone. But what we experience is a malign intent to deprive us. Within the paranoid-schizoid position, then, though it is the beginning of love, there is no point at which we recognize our carer as a whole person with her own needs and obligations outside our relationship with her. Instead, we know of two figures, one good and one evil. If the world is not actively nurturing us, we feel the world is actively attacking us. The paranoid position also gives us a way of understanding ourselves. In Klein's view, once we have projected goodness outside ourselves, we can introject goodness and identify ourselves with it. Loving oneself in the paranoid way has a big downside, however. It tends to intensify our projection of badness onto the outside world, and has us multiply the faults and evils we see in others, to try and make ourselves feel good.

Fortunately, the paranoid-schizoid position is not the end of the story. In the preferred, healthy course of events, we develop a second position during our first year of life. This is the 'depressive position' (Klein 1975b). When the baby feels safe enough to expect good things to happen and to take her carer for granted, she has less need of the stark division between good and bad and less need to keep judging the world. This makes it possible for the baby to recognize carers as whole people and to recognize that the world is often neutral toward her. From the depressive position, nothing is absolutely good and nothing is absolutely bad. When things do not go our way, we need not feel under attack, so we gain emotionally from the depressive position. But we also lose a great deal. There is no longer any absolute good in the world. The depressive position involves disappointment, grief and mourning for the loss of the absolutely benign and the loss of our experience, illusory though it was, of being the focus of absolutely benign attention.

Throughout the course of our lives and in changing circumstances, we switch between these two positions. Though both are available to us, at any given moment, one or other will be dominant. Often, when we feel most vulnerable, we turn to paranoia to give ourselves solace. The high-contrast world of the paranoid-schizoid position is attractive. It offers the experience of the absolutely benign, at the price of seeing others' neutrality toward us as hatred. When we adopt the depressive position, we gain a degree of emotional stability and coherence and can see the world far less judgementally. But there are losses here too. With no absolute good to introject, we see ourselves as mixtures of good and bad. An increasingly detached and realistic assessment of the world exposes us to guilt and to remorse for our own failings. For Klein (1975a, 1975b), psychological illness arises when we are not agile enough to switch between positions. Schizophrenia and clinical depression are the results of being stuck in one position or the other.

Parallels between Klein and Gilligan

I would suggest that if we read Klein's (1975a, 1975b) views in terms of attachment and separation, certain parallels between her work and Gilligan's (1982) emerge. The paranoid-schizoid position is one of tight attachment to and high involvement in one's milieu. Nothing can happen in the world without the mind formulating a powerful emotional response. Introspection is at a minimum, since the struggle over one's own value is conducted externally in terms of the value one grants or denies to others. Projection and introjection tie one tightly to one's milieu and to the persons that compose it. The depressive position is one of emotional detachment from one's milieu. In this position, one already knows that the world contains good and bad in mixtures, so one is relatively calm and non-judgemental about it. The psychological conflicts that typify the depressive position take place internally. Knowing oneself to be a mixture of good and bad, one experiences guilt for the bad. The key clinical question is whether, in the absence of absolute good, the depressive's remorse and reparations can ever outweigh the bad they carry inside them.

Clearly both Klein (1975a, 1975b) and Gilligan (1982) were concerned with morality and judgement, and both were in search of the psychological bases of human value and acts of human evaluation. There are great differences in the focus of their work, of course, but both women, in stark contrast to much that we have seen before, see human life as inevitably involving *both* attachment *and* separation. It is also clear for both of them that attachment and separation are phenomena that are in tension with one another. Distributed as a dynamic tension over time, they do not easily overlap. This relationship of switching-between and of ongoing, unresolved dynamic tension is one manifestation of separability. As I now turn to Winnicott (1971), it should become clear that separability can also be manifested in peaceful overlaps of attachment and separation. As I have suggested above, separability is not a thing, nor is it a relationship. It is, instead, the possibility of all manner of relationships between separation and attachment and between persons. It is the realm of actual possibility that lies between the twin fantasies of complete separation and complete embeddedness.

How does Winnicott differ from Klein?

Klein's account of the relationships humans strike with the world is a compelling one. It offers a vocabulary for describing and understanding an enormous range of feelings and reactions. The paranoid-schizoid position allows us to understand why others' indifference should ever bother us. It can also shed light on phenomena ranging from the mundane feeling that the world is against us, to the mutual blame and insult that lie at the heart of party-based democracy, each party trying to filthy the name of the other. Her account of the depressive position tells us that the price of balance and good sense is often to be paid in responsibility and guilt.

You may have noticed, however, that for Klein, there is no escape from bad feelings. After all, she even chose to call the more stable and realistic of her positions 'depressive'. At least one commentator (Gomez 1997) has noted a sharp contrast between Klein's overall pessimism and the far more optimistic tone that Winnicott adopts. Aware that Winnicott knew Klein very well, Gomez suggests that Winnicott's (1971) generally cheerful tone was an attempt on his part to compensate for Klein's (1975a, 1975b) sadness. This may or may not be the case. But, as I will now suggest, the differences between him and Klein are not restricted to emotional tone.

With any author, no matter how accomplished, it is always possible to take a step back from the way they present the world and ask how realistic their views are. We can ask, for example, whether anything is 'missing' from their account that we would expect or hope to see depicted. We can gauge the emphases authors give against our own view of things. If we perform this sort of exercise with Klein (1975a, 1975b), the results are quite striking. She presents us with powerful emotions, with patterns of thought that characterize her different 'positions' and with a few basic facts of life that are relevant to babies' experience. Her focus is on the inner world of the emotions so she has little to say about mundane material matters. Actual 'objects' like pillows, cups, clothes, toys, and so on, fill up the lives of adults and children, but Klein ignores them. She has good reason to ignore them. For her, they can only form a backdrop to the psychological drama of existence. However, while Winnicott has regard for infants' feelings of abandonment, in his view, infants have more resources at their disposal to manage these feelings than their patterns of thought alone. Mothers and other carers, for example, are not just present or absent. They also interact with their babies, holding, feeding, talking, singing and playing. For Winnicott, then, most mothers actively help their babies to deal with their feelings of abandonment. Further, babies and young children, at least in the minority world, are surrounded by material things to play with and to investigate. Winnicott is closely attuned to the human significance of objects in this mundane, material sense. For him, they help babies, and the rest of us, deal with experiences of separation and of attachment. The 'transitional' experience of moving between attachment and separation is managed with the help of 'transitional objects' and a whole broad class of 'transitional phenomena'.

Transitional objects

Here is Winnicott's description of a common practice of infants and children, one that is less common, but certainly not unknown, among adults:

> In common experience one of the following occurs, complicating an auto-erotic experience such as thumb-sucking:
> i) with the other hand the baby takes an external object, say a part of a sheet or blanket, into the mouth along with the fingers; or
> ii) somehow or other the bit of cloth is held and sucked, or not actually sucked; the objects used naturally include napkins and (later) handkerchiefs, and this depends on what is readily and reliably available.
>
> (1971: 3–4)

For Winnicott, thumb-sucking itself seems to need no further explanation than to be described as 'auto-erotic'. Babies suck their thumbs because they can and because it feels good. It feels good because, broadly speaking, it answers some of their instinctive desire. As a phenomenon, thumb-sucking comes as no surprise to anyone, like Winnicott, who has studied psycho-analytic literature, because, as he suggests, there is plenty of reference in this literature to 'the progress from "hand to mouth" to "hand to genital"' (Winnicott 1971: 3). In Winnicott's view, however, this same literature has very little, if anything, to say about the 'complication' of thumb-sucking through the introduction of sheets, blankets or other bits of cloth into the baby's routine. Winnicott was fascinated by babies' use of these objects, and, as he tried to analyse their use, he began to develop a fresh account of what humans can do when presented with issues of separation and attachment. Paranoid-schizoid and depressive positions do not exhaust the possibilities.

For Winnicott, babies' relationships with their object of choice, be it a cloth or a toy, have a number of special qualities:

1   'The infant assumes rights over the object, and we agree to this assumption. Nevertheless, some abrogation of omnipotence is a feature from the start' (Winnicott 1971: 5). This means that the infant will complain if the object is taken away from them, and that 'we' grown-ups and carers tend to respect the infant's implicit claim of owner-ship. In this way carers help to sustain the infant's possession of the object.

2   'The object is affectionately cuddled as well as excitedly loved and mutilated ... It must survive instinctual loving, and also hating and, if it be a feature, pure aggression' (Winnicott 1971: 5). This means

that the infant not only possesses the object, but also that its possession is highly emotionally charged, involving feelings of wanting to be close to the object and feelings of wanting to reject it.

3   'It must never change, unless changed by the infant ... it must seem to the infant to give warmth, or to move, or to have texture, or to do something that seems to show that it has vitality or reality of its own' (Winnicott 1971: 5). This means that if the object is removed by a carer, say, for washing, the infant may become angry or distressed. If it is then returned to the infant, clean, the infant will feel that something vital has been removed from it. As Winnicott writes of such objects, 'parents get to know its value and carry it round when travelling. The mother lets it get dirty and even smelly, knowing that by washing it she introduces a break in continuity in the infant's experience, a break that may destroy the meaning and value of the object to the infant' (1971: 4).

Why do babies and children form these relationships with objects? Why does the dirtiness and smelliness of the objects matter so much? Recall Klein's (1975a, 1975b) account of the problems that a baby faces. Warmth and security come and go. This makes babies anxious and, in these conditions, they respond by creating the fantasies of the paranoid-schizoid position. For Klein, babies' defensive response to anxiety takes place within their minds and only within their minds because their minds are the only resource they have to work with. It is precisely because they cannot control external reality that they fall back on elaborating their internal reality. For Klein (1975a, 1975b), therefore, we have, all of us, been set the problem of how to match up internal and external realities, the problem of how to bring them into balance. But Klein missed two things that Winnicott noticed. Not all babies have to work out their anxieties without the insightful help of their carers and not all babies have to work out their anxieties without physical props.

Even though Winnicott agrees that internal and external realities exist, that they frequently stand in contradiction to each other and that the acceptance of external reality is an on-going challenge for us all (1971: 13), he does not believe that human experience is exhausted by the two terms 'internal' and 'external'. It is his view that the discussion of and understanding of 'experience' requires us to consider 'the third part of the life of a human being ... an intermediate area of experiencing, to which inner reality and external life both contribute' (1971: 2). Babies invest so much in their transitional objects because these objects are part of a novel way of managing separation anxieties. Where the paranoid-schizoid position manages anxiety by letting the internal world overwrite the external world and where the depressive position surrenders the internal world to the terms of the external world, the strategy that interests Winnicott depends for its effectiveness on blurring the difference between the internal psychological world and the external world of interaction with real people.

The baby's special relationship with a transitional object, a relationship supported and acknowledged by carers, allows the baby temporarily to ignore problems of attachment to and separation from the world. In the paranoid-schizoid position the problem is that the external world lets you down. In the depressive position, the problem is that the inner life lets the external world down. But a transitional object places the very grounds of these problems, the difference between inside and outside, in suspension. It is able to do this because, for the child, the transitional object is never simply part of the external world and never simply part of herself. It is at this point that the curious matter of the dirtiness and smelliness of the object becomes crucial. If the object has a smell of its own and a texture of its own, then it can be seen as having a life or 'vitality' (Winnicott 1971: 4) of its own. In this sense, it stands independent of the baby. Yet the object acquired its smell and some of its texture while it was being used by the baby. So the smell also marks the object out as part of, as belonging to, the baby. In the baby's experience, the object is both separate from and attached to her. As with Winnicott's piece of string, transitional objects achieve attachment and separation simultaneously. Likewise, the transitional object blurs the distinction between 'inside' and 'outside'. When the child reaches for the object for comfort, the object brings that comfort from the outside. Yet, it can also be treated by the child as nothing more than a passive screen for the projection of her internal emotional states. The object may be beaten or discarded just as often as it is cuddled. It is also important to note that the transitional object is the result of the coordinated activity of the child and of her carers. Without carers' implicit understanding of the importance of the object for the baby, the proper relationship could not be sustained. Thus not only are the boundaries between inside and outside suspended around the transitional object, but it is also clear that this suspension is consensual. As Winnicott puts it:

> Of the transitional object it can be said that it is a matter of agree-
> ment between us and the baby that we will never ask the question:
> 'Did you conceive of this or was it presented to you from without?'
> The important point is that no decision on this point is expected.
> The question is not to be formulated.
>
> (1971: 12)

Winnicott makes it quite clear that not all babies are fortunate enough to enjoy such support. For the majority who do, transitional objects help them manage separation anxieties. The minority who do not enjoy carers' support in this matter are quite likely to suffer.

Transitional phenomena and separability

So far I have examined Winnicott's (1971) analysis of a behaviour pattern common to many babies and children. I have also suggested that Winnicott offers a novel view of babies' response to separation, one that takes into account the facts that babies are more than just minds and that they interact with their physical and social surroundings. Equipped with a transitional object, babies never have to face their 'separateness' from the external world alone. The transitional object is a part of the external world, so it is separate from them, but at the same time, they participate in its being and they and their carers have marked it out as belonging to them. Where logic would suggest that an object must be either internal or external, either a psychological or physical object, the transitional object is both/and. For Winnicott, then, the transitional object is both an ontological cushion, which softens any clash between the baby's internal and external realities, and an ontological safe passage between internal and external realities. But how do transitional objects relate to my term 'separability'?

In the introduction to this chapter I distinguished between the *temporal* patterns that separability allows, such as the ongoing tension or dialectic (Gilligan 1982) between separation and attachment, and the *spatial* patterns that separability allows, where partial separation and partial attachment overlap one another without tension or conflict. Transitional objects are a good example of the latter. The transitional object is both part of the baby and not part of the baby, and, according to Winnicott, this paradox is essential to it and to its functioning. As he writes, 'the difficult part of the theory of the transitional object ... is that a paradox is involved which needs to be accepted, tolerated and not resolved' (1971: 53). Like so many matters of human value (Serres 1991), the transitional object does not conform to the logical principle of the excluded middle. But there is more to be said about the relationship between transitional objects and separability.

If Winnicott had stopped thinking just after his discussion of the transitional objects of infancy, we would have been able to draw a simple conclusion about his work. We could have concluded that for Winnicott, transitional objects mark a phase in human life, a period of transition during which growing babies need cushioning from the harsh reality of separation. We could further have concluded that once this transitional period is over, the phenomenon disappears. This would place Winnicott in sympathy with all those who place such a high value on the clarity of psychological independence, those who think that the 'individual' as a cultural-psychological form is based on the achievement of separation. If this were the case, then Winnicott would provide no alternative vision of human value to the individualism which measures our worth by our distance from the historical past, from our embodiment, from our natal and family relations, and ultimately, from our childhoods. But Winnicott (1971) does not stop there. He suggests that, for those of us lucky enough to enjoy psychological well-being, separability remains a vital facet of experience throughout our lives.

For the majority of children, the importance of the first transitional object decreases as they grow. But, for Winnicott this is not because they have finally achieved a clear, firm separation between internal and external realities, nor is it because they have finally realized the sense and superiority of independence from the world. On Winnicott's (1971) view, no-one is ever done with the business of separating from and re-attaching to the world. Instead, as children grow, they extend the special qualities of the first transitional object over a whole field of transitional phenomena. Winnicott finds examples of transitional phenomena wherever the value of an activity requires the suspension of such questions as 'is this activity taking place in my imagination or in the real world?'; and, 'is this activity "pretend" or "real"?'

Many examples of transitional phenomena can be found in children's play. For example, a toy may be given a voice of its own and marched about as if it were moving under its own power. Though this sort of play is imaginative and thus 'belongs' to the inner, psychological world, it needs to involve real objects so it also 'belongs' to the external, physical world. Story-telling involves a suspension of the difference between 'pretend' and 'real'. A good story-teller does not just read out the words, but tries to embody and enliven characters with a range of voices. Many children's stories involve actions and rhymes that can be performed by teller and audience. These help to bring the pretend content of the story into present physical reality. The first transitional object is not the sign of a passing phase, but is a seed of separability that can grow into an appreciation of the myriad human activities that can take place when issues of inside and outside, privacy and participation, separation and attachment are successfully suspended. Just as the infant needs carers to help in the creation of a transitional object, so transitional phenomena in general depend on consensus and collective action. A simple illustration of this can be found in live theatre where successful performance depends on the audience's suspension of disbelief.

For Winnicott (1971), the whole sphere of human cultural production is imbued with the characteristics of transitional phenomena. This includes games and sports, religious practice and experience, and art and creativity. The value of these activities is created within a consensual transitional zone. Their 'mysteries' reflect this. What real value can football have when its points and penalties are distributed according to fabricated rules? If a monotheistic believer cannot point to their God, why do they value their faith so much? How can paint on a canvas translate into millions of dollars? The first transitional object is a seed of separability that can grow into a participation in worlds of human value that suspend the difference between imagination and reality.

Play and well-being

Given what I have covered so far, it would be easy to forget that Winnicott was a practising psychotherapist. Part of his job was to distinguish between psychological health and illness and to help people to transform their lives. One of the key concepts he developed to give expression to his practice was the 'false self'. Before I discuss this and contrast it with Winnicott's (1971) vision of psychological well-being, I will need to outline a few consequences of transitional phenomena. These consequences take the form of three statements that are formally self-contradictory but that capture certain vital features of human value.

1 *I am my body and I am not.* I have argued that we should see the first transitional object as a seed of separability. Let me expand on this. Caring for a baby involves a great deal of attention to the baby as a body. This body must be fed and cleaned, moved about and supported. When babies develop a first transitional object, they develop something that is part of themselves but is not identical to themselves. It is both an extension of their body and something separate from their body. When carers recognize and respect a transitional object, what is being recognized and respected? From an adult carer's point of view, caring for a transitional object is an indirect way of caring for the baby. Respecting the object means respecting the baby's feelings. From babies' point of view something subtly different is happening. Having their special relationship respected means that their ability on occasion to extend what they think of as 'themselves' through physical space is acknowledged and respected. This means that it feels safe for babies to see themselves as more than just their body. It is not only babies who need to have this sense of sometimes being more than their bodies. The guarantee that one both is and is not one's body is a fundamental basis for participation in social life. Many prevalent forms of prejudice and disrespect, such as racism, sexism, and hostility towards the physically disabled and elderly, involve reducing people to their bodies. Thus transitional objects are a seed of separability from one's body that enables social participation.

2 *I belong to my carer and I do not.* As I have noted, babies and young children experience a great deal of dependency on their carers. This means that their carers have a high degree of control over them.

Issues of possession and self-possession therefore crop up in many mundane situations including feeding, getting dressed and going to the toilet. Many carers and children find themselves in conflict over these issues. For example, children who prefer to play rather than to eat at a designated meal-time will often find their carers becoming increasingly insistent that they eat *now*. Children who do not want to put on a coat when leaving the house on a cold day may find themselves being coerced into wearing the coat. According to Winnicott (1971), the transitional object is the child's first possession. As such, it forms a model for the child's growing sense of self-possession and desire for self-determination. As we have seen, the transitional object is both part of and not part of the child. If children are lucky, this ambivalence of possession helps them and their carers to negotiate possessiveness and control. Without the ambivalence of separability, however, the relationship between child and carer can only be resolved by one party or the other losing outright. If the parent loses, the child will, in all likelihood, not be adequately cared for. If children lose, they will suffer the fate of continually surrendering their self-determination to external control.

3   *I am part of the social world and I am not.* As Winnicott (1971) suggests, the transitional object is both part of the child's private, internal world and, in its physicality and separability from the child, part of public, external reality. Much the same can be said of transitional phenomena in general. Cultural phenomena are both private and public. They form a sphere of activity in which the child can belong to and participate in social activity, while also reserving a space of withdrawal. Thus, when children are playing or singing a song, they can participate in social life without fear that the many rules, mores and customs that make up social interaction will invade and dominate their private, internal world.

Each of the three statements above about children who are enjoying transitional phenomena has its counterpart in adult life. First, as I have suggested, it is important for us all to identify with our bodies, yet not to be reduced to and identified solely with our bodies. Thus, in adult life, 'I am this body and I am not'. If we are capable of loyalty and yet are capable of questioning those we are loyal to, we never simply 'belong' to a person, family, institution or nation. So we can say 'I do belong to this person/family/institution and I do not'. Regarding our participation in social life, we will often feel a need to observe convention, but also sometimes feel a need to question it. In this sense 'I am obliged to follow convention and I am not'. Just as Winnicott's (1971) understanding of a happy infancy involves ambiguity and separability, so a healthy adult life needs a well-developed transitional zone. Given that internal private realities often differ from public external realities, given that our desires and feelings are not always mirrored by our circumstances, we need transitional phenomena to give us 'wiggle-room'. Without them, life would be an unremitting and exhausting conflict between inner and outer realities. Winnicott uses this insight to interpret two forms of psychological distress. He interprets 'psychosis' as a condition in which, for want of a transitional zone, conflict between inner and outer realities has been resolved in favour of the inner world of imagination. Where people experience the world as drained of meaning or where they are weakened by lacking a stable sense of self, Winnicott would suggest that the external world of convention and social mores has won out. People who adopt a conformist 'false self' (Winnicott 1971: 14) and psychotics are both suffering from an inability to play, to move safely and confidently between separateness from and attachment to external social realities.

Conclusion

For Winnicott, living in pure separation is madness and living in pure attachment is the living death of the false self. All that stands between us and these frightening alternatives are transitional phenomena, the 'both/and' of separability that cushions conflicts and forms a safe passage of communication between private and public realities. It might seem as if we are therefore in quite a predicament, protected from profound psychological suffering only by a set of phenomena that involve self-contradiction and that do not bear logical scrutiny. If we insist on applying logic to Winnicott's (1971) account of human value, all we will see in transitional phenomena is a slender thread of nonsense like his paradoxical length of string. But if we accept that partial separation and partial attachment may co-exist and overlap in peace, we will see that the field of transitional phenomena is vast, incorporating all areas of human creativity, including religious experience, artistic production, games and play. All of this stems from our first possessive relation with the material world in the shape of the transitional object. Whether that object was a cloth, a toy or a song, the ambiguities of the relationship allowed us an autonomous yet intimate involvement with the material world.

Just as Gilligan (1982) has shown us that it is possible to understand childhood and human value through separabilities that are distributed over time, so Winnicott (1971) focuses on separabilities distributed in the spatial overlap of internal and external reality. Neither asserts actual and complete separation as the standard of human life. Neither asserts total embeddedness or attachment as the fundamental human reality. Both have helped me to clarify separability as the possibility of relationship. It seems, then, that there are grounds on which human value can be based that will not lead to separation anxieties in the face of children's rights. Perhaps in the future they will form part of our stock of common sense.

PART 4
COMPETENCE AND SEPARABILITY

In my argument so far, I have found it necessary to write against the possibility of actual and complete separation. I have taken examples of apparent separation, and I have reduced them to 'performances of separateness' that rely for their effectiveness on a systematic inattention to separability. I have then asserted separability both as a condition that is logically prior to separateness and, more importantly, as a condition that should be prior to separateness in our understanding of the sources of human value. I have made these points because, as I argued in Part 1, a lack of awareness of separability creates unwarranted anxieties about and resistances to children's rights. At this point I would like to discuss a few more features of my strategy.

Following Gilligan (1982) and Winnicott (1971), I have avoided taking up the cause of various opposites of actual and complete separation such as 'attachment', 'connection' and 'dependency'. Instead, using Gilligan (1982) and Winnicott (1971) to illustrate ideas of partial separation and partial attachment, I have tried to reveal and to highlight the ways in which separability informs the creation of human value. Like Gilligan, I have not adopted a strategy of simply inverting an old hierarchy. I have not sought to replace a fixation on separation with a fixation on attachment. Gilligan always had the option of countering the masculine bias of much moral discourse by arguing that the moral voice of 'care', associated with women, is in some way superior to that of 'justice', associated with men. Instead, she found a way to accept both voices and went on to imagine what the relationship between them might be like. I am taking a similar approach to the controversy over children's rights and self-possession. Children are often understood as being too 'weak' to have rights, to possess themselves and to speak for themselves. When measured against a standard of human value that is based on actual and complete separation, their unconcealed dependencies and connectedness conventionally disqualify them from full human value. They cannot be treated 'as individuals' because, it seems, they are not proper individuals. I have the option of countering this chain of reasoning by offering an intellectual demolition of 'separateness' and of the figure of the 'individual'. I could try to level the ground between adults and children by arguing that despite the appearance of adult separateness and independence, everyone in fact, regardless of age, is equally embedded in utter dependency, on each other, on family, on institutions, etc. Indeed, my portrayal of actual and complete separateness as a 'performance' goes some way down this path. To follow this path all the way would be to purge myself of all age-based hierarchy, to replace the independent, separate figure that has long been the gold standard of human value with an injunction to value everyone equally. All should be valued, but none valued as individuals.

It is at this point that the notion of separability really comes into its own. It might be comforting to argue for the abolition of hierarchy and even intellectually stimulating to imagine a world in which there were no individuals, where performances of separateness were not called for. Marxist (Marx and Engels 1998) and feminist utopias (Gilman 1992), for example, have advanced the hope that we might one day acknowledge and respect our mutual connections and dependencies by adopting communal ways of living. At least one science fiction writer has imagined such an inverted world, a world in which the phrase 'egoizing propertarian' is at once an insult and an accusation of criminality (Le Guin 2003). Given the nature of my project, however, I cannot indulge this urge to reverse hierarchy, to dissolve arrogant separation in a warm bath of connections. My aim is to alter common-sense patterns of thought and feeling around children's rights so that children may more easily enjoy partial separation from the adults who surround them, whenever they require it. I could not call for this while simultaneously asserting the primacy of 'connection' or 'embeddedness'.

As I argued in Chapter 1, children's rights become controversial whenever they involve children and their interests, opinions, desires and voices being considered as separable from those of the parents, wider family, communities and political states that surround them. These are the points at which an inspection of circumstances conducted from the child's point of view can reveal whether the relationship between the child and those who surround her is mutually beneficial or whether that relationship needs to change. Clearly, if I tried to lay an ethic of indiscriminate mutual dependency and connection across these circumstances, I would remove the possibility of inspecting relationships from the child's point of view. Like everybody else, the child would have no distinct 'point of view'. Unless we allow that children are separable from those who surround them, and unless we make sure that they can on occasion mark themselves and their viewpoints out against their background and environment, it would be hard indeed to get to grips with the moral and political differences and similarities between, for example, children in domestic slavery and children involved in other forms of unpaid domestic labour.

For reasons that I hope have been made clear, none of the above means that we have to return to the ideal of actual and complete separation that I have spent so much time distancing myself from. But it does bring back into focus a set of issues that I have so far skirted around. Adult separation anxieties are often expressed by questioning children's competence to wield rights and to wield rights responsibly. Given their lowly station in the developmental hierarchy, it is often thought that children would make a mess of rights. This view itself plays a part in intensifying the very anxieties that make it seem so compelling and commonsensical. This observation, however, should not lead us hastily to dismiss all questions of competence and responsibility. There are two closely related problems here. First, if children are to be deemed capable of deploying rights, they must be thought capable of thinking for themselves. Second, if children are to be deemed fit to deploy rights, they must be deemed capable of using those rights responsibly. Even though I have presented arguments against measuring human value with the fictitious standard of actual and complete separation and even though I have clarified separability and its place in shaping human value, I have yet to examine the ideas of thinking for oneself and of acting responsibly with self-control from the perspective of separability. These problems are fundamental for anyone who is interested in children's place in society. Assumptions about them shape such matters as the age of political majority in democracies and what 'freedom' is allowed to mean for the young.

'Thinking for oneself' and 'self-control' would seem to lie at the heart of actual and complete separation. They are the cognitive and moral tokens of independence and trustworthiness that many contemporary adults strive to possess. But can they be understood in a way that is compatible with separability? Can they be wrested from the set of mystifications that surround the figure of the independent individual? If they can, then children's exclusion from the status of full, rights-bearing people on the grounds of competence will look less like common sense. It is at this point that I turn to the work of the psychologist Lev Vygotsky (1986) and the sociologist Norbert Elias (1994) for assistance.

7 Lev Vygotsky
Thinking for oneself

Introduction

How well does the psychologist Lev Vygotsky (1986) fit among the other authors in the range I have chosen to discuss, those developmental thinkers of the mid-twentieth century who wrote in the shadow of Freud (1963) and Piaget (1927)? He was, after all, born in 1896, the same year as Piaget. He was hardly a mid-twentieth-century figure in a chronological sense. Growing up in early twentieth-century Russia, his intellectual development was strongly influenced by Marxism. He died young, before the drawbacks of the Soviet system became obvious. Vygotsky nevertheless came 'after' Piaget in the sense that he often defined his work and reported his findings in opposition to Piagetian views. By the time Vygotsky first published his *Thought and Language* in 1934, Piaget was already well established. In this chapter, I will compare and contrast Vygotsky's (1986) and Piaget's (1927) theories of development. I will interpret them both as accounts of 'thinking for oneself'. I am taking 'thinking for oneself' as my theme because, as I suggested above, it is, according to common sense, the cognitive component of the competence to wield rights. It is a faculty that children are often assumed to lack and adults are assumed to possess.

As with previous comparisons I have made between developmental thinkers (see Chapter 5), it is not my aim in this chapter to show that Vygotsky is right and Piaget is wrong. I offer no experimental evidence in favour of or against either. Indeed, some contemporary psychologists would have it that differences of opinion between Piaget and Vygotsky need not concern us at all, since decades of empirical and theoretical work have rendered them both irrelevant (Gopnik and Meltzoff 1998). I am happy to leave the business of producing scientifically authoritative statements about child development to contemporary psychologists. I will be arguing, however, that Vygotsky (1986) has something distinctive to offer the field of common-sense understandings of development and competence. I will suggest that if Vygotsky's (1986) account of the development of 'mind' is taken for granted in the future, just as Piaget's (1927) is today, children's rights will no longer seem a threatening prospect.

As is the way with many commonsensical ideas, adults' ability to 'think for themselves' is rarely analysed or understood as in need of explanation. One is either taken to possess this quality, or one is taken to lack it. As some contemporary sociologists of childhood would suggest, however (James et al. 1998), if we dig a little deeper, a fairly clear, culturally dominant account of 'thinking for oneself' is available. In this account 'thinking for oneself' is a point that is reached after a lengthy process of transcendence or struggle for independence. This process or struggle is typically taken to involve the transcendence of one's environment through one's own effort, often in the face of opposition from that environment. This account has parallels with broader notions of independence of mind. For example, the philosopher Kant writing about 'enlightenment' around the time of the French Revolution, defined 'enlightenment' as a practice of thinking for oneself. He offered this enlightened practice as a revolutionary antidote to traditional forms of knowledge, such as institutionalized religious belief and as an antidote to accepting the beliefs of the powerful as one's own. As he saw it, the risky business of questioning tradition and authority will eventually result in independence of mind and freedom of action. Kant (1983) explicitly compared the condition of the unenlightened with the condition of childhood. For Piaget (1927), children 'think for themselves' from an early age, trying to make sense of the world with their own theories, 'reprogramming' their own minds in response to the environment. Unfortunately, until they have gone through a long process of assimilating and accommodating to experience, their thinking is 'wrong' in the sense that it is a poor reflection of the true nature of the world and their place in it. For Piaget, thinking for oneself and getting it right is a point that is reached in the course of becoming rational.

In this chapter, following Vygotsky (1986), I will develop the view that thinking for oneself is a process that goes on, and goes on changing, from the early years. On this point Vygotsky and Piaget are agreed. However, the two authors differ over the role of other people as aspects of the developing child's environment. For Piaget, children have to do all the work of development themselves, while for Vygotsky, the labour of development is always shared. This is because Piaget's development is primarily cognitive, taking place within the mind, while Vygotsky's development is about linkages between physical and social activity and cognition. I will also argue that Piaget and Vygotsky have rather different views of what children have to come to terms with as they learn about the world. For Piaget, reality demands of us that, ultimately, we adopt and conform to certain well-defined philosophical commitments. In contrast, for Vygotsky, reality is most commonly experienced as a series of practical problems requiring practical, rather than philosophical solutions. This difference is crucial to questions of development and human value. Where Piaget thinks of development on the model of a school curriculum, Vygotsky treats it as rather more wild. I will begin with Vygotsky's (1986) critical account of Piaget's (1927) work.

Autistic, egocentric and directed thought

In Chapter 2, I spent some time presenting Piaget's (1927) concept of 'ego-centrism'. You may recall that he saw children under 7 or 8 years old as egocentric thinkers. This did not mean that these children were self-centred, rather that they were not fully aware that they were separate from others. This failure to appreciate separateness, which for Piaget is a central truth of human existence, continues to structure children's thinking even as they develop. Magical thinking and a sense of 'participation' or superstitious connection with the world only recede when the lessons of life have fully convinced them of certain views best described as 'philosophical'. These include the beliefs that:

- each of us is separated from the world and from other people by a clear boundary which defines the limits of our mind and the scope of its powers;
- there is a sharp and knowable difference between fantasy and reality;
- thought, desire or fantasy cannot influence real events without an intermediary such as language.

For Piaget, these beliefs happen to be correct. They are what the world teaches the growing mind. This much is familiar, but Vygotsky (1986) tells us something new about Piaget's work. He argues that, for Piaget (1959), ego-centric thought is not the child's first and original form of thought. He shows that Piaget supposes that another form of thought, called 'autistic thought', comes first and that egocentric thought follows, forming a bridge to 'directed' thought.

'Directed thought' is just another term for fully developed reason. As Piaget puts it:

> Directed thought is conscious, i.e., it pursues an aim which is present to the mind of the thinker; it is intelligent, which means it is adapted to reality and tries to influence it; it admits of being true or false (empirically or logically true), and it can be communicated by language.
>
> (1959: 43)

From Piaget's point of view, egocentric thought is certainly strange, but it does at least represent an attempt to get to grips with reality through 'parti-cipation'. For him, autistic thought involves no such attempt. It is like a sealed chamber of incommunicable fantasy:

> Autistic thought is subconscious, which means that the aims it pursues and the problems it tries to solve are not present in consciousness; it is not adapted to reality, but creates for itself a dream world of imagination; it tends, not to establish truths, but to satisfy desires, and it remains strictly individual and incommunicable as such by means of language.
>
> (Piaget 1959: 43)

When considering Piaget's 'autistic' thought, it is best to avoid trying to map it onto today's understandings of the spectrum of autistic conditions (Attwood 1997). As his use of the word 'subconscious' above suggests, Piaget's (1959) model of autistic thought derives instead from Freud's distinction between the irrational 'pleasure principle' which governs subconscious mental activity and the rational 'reality principle' that governs the conscious mind.

According to Vygotsky (1986), then, Piaget supposes that there are three main kinds of thought. The original form of thought is autistic. It has no goal other than the satisfaction of desire through fantasy. Since it is unable to measure itself against reality, and since it cannot be communicated in language, it has no relationship with the outside world at all. Egocentric thought is an advance on autistic thought in the sense that it can address the outside world, but it addresses the outside world as if there were no difference between insides and outsides, with the consequence that children often believe things to be the truth that they have merely imagined. Directed thought involves interaction between mind and world that is governed by an awareness of the fact of the separation of mind and world. Thought originates with autism and develops direction, passing through egocentrism on the way. Vygotsky (1986) admits that Piaget (1959) never presented this succession of types of thought systematically, but he insists that the journey through the three forms is the 'cornerstone of his whole theoretical edifice' (Vygotsky 1986: 20). Having made this point, Vygotsky then begins to raise some difficult questions.

Is autistic thought the first form of thought?

As I suggested in Chapter 2, it is very hard to imagine what forms of evidence Piaget (1959) could have drawn on to test his hypotheses about the very earliest forms of thought. As we shall see shortly, he did provide evidence for the existence of egocentrism in young children. If we share his interpretation of that evidence, we might be inclined to follow the path of reasoning that led him to posit autistic thought as the most basic and original form. I will shortly explain why Vygotsky did not share Piaget's (1959) interpretation of that evidence for egocentrism and I will describe his alternative interpretation in full. Vygotsky (1986) began his critique of Piaget's (1959) account of development, however, by offering some theoretical arguments intended to discredit the idea that autistic thought is the origin of thought. By doing this, Vygotsky attempted to shatter the clear line of developmental progress that Piaget had established from autistic to directed thought. As I will later explain, to the extent that Vygotsky successfully disrupts Piaget's (1959) account of the place of each type of thought in the lifecourse, he also makes way for an account of 'thinking for oneself' that is compatible with separability.

Vygotsky begins his critique by drawing on another author, Bleuler (1912). Bleuler could not accept Piaget's (1959) views on autism, and was equally suspicious of Freud's pleasure principle as a primary psychic structure. He simply did not find it credible that imagination could provide any form of satisfaction for an infant. Why suppose that we begin with a closed circuit of imaginary desire and imaginary satisfaction that excludes and ignores the outside world, when babies are notorious for crying? As Bleuler puts it, 'I do not see a hallucinatory satisfaction in a baby, but I do see a satisfaction after the actual intake of food' (1912: 26–7). We might defend Piaget from Bleuler and Vygotsky's incredulity by pointing out that he is quite clear that autistic thought is of no practical use and that is why the developing child transcends it. Piaget might further clarify his position by saying that though there is no match between activities in the real world and the contents of the baby's mind, the baby's mind nevertheless is full of fantastical self-gratification and contains this activity precisely because of the lack of relationship between the inside of the baby's mind and the real world. But we may still ask Piaget, and Freud for that matter, for positive reasons why we should suppose that an autistic carousel of self-gratification spins within each baby.

Vygotsky (1986) does not offer us an explicit account of why Piaget (1959) found the hypothesis of original autism so attractive. Perhaps this is where the connection between 'level of development' and human value that was forged with the term 'primitive' (see Chapter 2) makes its strongest impression on Piaget. Within the prejudices of his times, all 'primitives', including children, 'savages' and women, were to be closely monitored. It was thought that since they lack the guiding light of reason, they were always likely to surrender to desire. Piaget's interest in a primordial and ineffectual autism, posited as a condition to be transcended, might be the mark of this set of associations. Alternatively, it could be that as the socio-cultural figure of the individual arose in modern European life, so a fear of the dangers of its isolation and new-found freedoms of imagination also grew. If this was the case, then Piaget's association of autism with early life could be read as a sign of a general cultural anxiety of the following form: unless you take care to adapt yourself to socially sanctioned reality, you will fall back into a solipsistic world of your own imaginings from which there is no escape. The most charitable reading of Piaget's (1959) confident assertion of original autism is that it derives from his particular method of interpreting data. Piaget was an extraordinarily empathic psychologist. When he had talked to children and asked them searching questions about the world, he pored over these data trying to reconstruct the unifying principles that underlay any peculiarities in their answers. His concern was always to determine how the world must look to his research participants, given their answers to his questions. Apply the same method of empathic interpretation to an unborn or just new-born child, whose senses are as yet relatively uninformative, and, perhaps, if you think there must be thought, it must be autistic.

The second problem Vygotsky (1986) raises is based on evolutionary links between humans and animals. If autism comes first in each human life, what evolutionary pressures could have given rise to it? As Bleuler puts it, 'Animal psychology ... knows only the reality function' (1912: 26–27). Given that selective pressures are likely to favour only those creatures who are oriented to survival, and given that survival requires a tendency to prefer real food over imaginary food, why would autism evolve as the origin of thought? These two objections, of course, do not disprove Piaget's (1959) hypothesis of original autism. But they do raise the question of why Piaget believed, wanted or needed autism to be the first step. In the following section, I will suggest, with Vygotsky (1986), that Piaget needed autism to come first so as to stabilize his interpretation of data about older children's speech, specifically his claim that children's psychology is fundamentally different from that of adults.

Egocentric speech?

One result of Vygotsky's (1986) awkward questions about original autism is to place children's egocentrism in question as well. In Vygotsky's view, Piaget (1959) has egocentric thought grow out of and supersede autistic thought. If evidence consistent with egocentrism can be found in children's behaviour, and if we, like Vygotsky, are not prepared to accept the hypothesis of original autism, what then are we to make of this evidence? This is precisely the situation that Vygotsky engineers for us as he turns to examine Piaget's interpretation of empirical data about children's speech.

We tend to think of speech as a means of communicating from one mind to another. This assumption is consistent with the set of approved philosophical positions I attributed to Piaget above. Sometimes, however, we can observe people apparently talking to themselves. What are they doing? Since this activity has no place within the approved philosophy of communication, it is often interpreted as the result of agitation, confusion, loss of control, or indeed, mental illness. One consistent finding of Piaget's (1959) research was that children younger than about 7 or 8 tended to speak to themselves a good deal more often than adults. For Piaget (1959), this was the principal sign of the egocentricity of their thought. He wrote: 'This talk is egocentric . . . chiefly because [the child] does not attempt to place himself at the point of view of his hearer . . . the child talks to himself as though he were thinking aloud. He does not address anyone' (Piaget 1959: 9)

Being self-referential, this form of speech is reminiscent of the inwardness of autistic thought. Thus, even though Piaget had no direct evidence of original autism, his interpretation of egocentric speech helped him make his hypothesis of original autism seem plausible. In order to use these data to shore up his theory of development, it was necessary for Piaget to interpret instances of children talking to themselves as a throwback to an earlier stage of development and as an activity that plays no positive role in their future development. On this view, it is something that we should see wither away as the child moves toward directed thought.

You may have had occasion to observe children talking to themselves. Picture a school playground with a painted line of squares, each square numbered '1 . . . 2 . . . 3 . . . etc.'. A 4-year-old girl jumps from square to square, counting as she goes. Her chant is egocentric in the sense that it is not directed toward an audience. But already, considering this example, we can, perhaps, begin to differ with Piaget (1959). The girl's chant is easily read not as a trace of an old, autistic, mistaken mind-set, but as a positive developmental activity. She is practising counting and having fun. Vygotsky (1986) offers us further examples and further fresh interpretations of instances of apparent egocentrism.

When Vygotsky replicated some of Piaget's studies, he also found a high level of egocentric speech in young children and he found that the older the children, the lower the incidence of egocentric speech. In one study he presented children with coloured pencils and paper and asked them to draw. He found that when the children were asked to draw a picture in a certain colour and were not provided with a pencil of that colour, their speech became more egocentric. As he writes: 'We found that in these difficult situations, the coefficient of egocentric speech almost doubled, in comparison with Piaget's normal figure for the same age and also in comparison with our figure for children not facing these problems' (Vygotsky 1986: 30). Vygotsky's alternative interpretation of egocentric speech flows from his assessment of the content of this speech. For example, a child asked to draw in blue but not given a blue pencil says to himself, 'Where's the pencil? I need a blue pencil. Never mind, I'll draw with the red one and wet it with water; it will become dark and look like blue' (Vygotsky 1986: 30). In Vygotsky's view, this child is using spoken language to help structure his thinking when dealing with the problem in front of him. There is a parallel here with the 4-year-old girl jumping and counting. She uses the painted boxes to structure her counting activity, just like Vygotsky's child uses spoken language. Once we grasp the activities and problems that young children are involved in when they are speaking to themselves, the view that they are doing nothing of developmental value becomes less credible, as does the hypothesis of original autism.

Language as technology

When discussing Bernstein's (1971) socio-linguistic studies in Chapter 3, I remarked that language is a very flexible technology. Its uses are not limited to communicating between minds that are otherwise separate from one another. Individual separation is just one of the performances that language allows. As Bernstein (1971) showed, when it takes the form of 'public language', it can also play a part in emphasizing the collective nature of thought, understanding and judgement over the individual nature of thought, understanding and judgement. In Vygotsky's (1986) interpretation of egocentric thought, language has the features of a tool designed for shaping and regulating thought, a tool to help us solve the many practical problems that present themselves to us in everyday life. Clearly, using language in this way is at variance with the philosophical premises that Piaget (1927) thinks the world schools us all in as we develop. Seen through those premises, talking to oneself is pointless. One cannot give oneself information that one already has. But when Vygotsky (1986) attends to the content rather than the form of egocentric speech, its value becomes clear.

Egocentric speakers are not involved in communication with another mind. But nor are they involved in magical thinking. Egocentric speakers do not necessarily believe that their words have a 'participative' power to influence the world. Nevertheless, their minds, bodies and powers of speech are all involved in a busy commerce with their environment as they manipulate pencil and paper, assess the problem that faces them, and arrive at a solution. This commerce has little respect for the clarity of the boundary between the 'inner' psychic world and the outer 'real' world. Vygotsky's (1986) child who is equipped only with a blue pencil is first drawn out of himself by a problem, then speaks the problem to himself, clarifying it and making it his own. He finds language a useful resource in dealing with that problem. He may or may not have inched himself closer to directed, rational thought, but if he has not, would it be right to declare that he had not developed? Would it be right to declare that he was not thinking for himself and getting the answer right?

From egocentric speech to private speech

So far it seems that Vygotsky (1986) has produced a fresh interpretation of children's egocentric speech. His interpretation turns Piaget's (1959) interpretation on its head. Where Piaget sees the signs of young children's failure properly to think for themselves, Vygotsky finds abundant evidence of their success in their egocentric speech. Where Piaget thinks of egocentric speech as a throwback to original autism, Vygotsky thinks of it as an example of children's use of language as a tool or technology to structure their thinking. There is, however, a further piece of evidence that Vygotsky needs to account for. Just like Piaget, he found that the older the children were, the more communicative and the less egocentric their speech tended to be.

Piaget already had an explanation for the decline of egocentric speech. His explanation is consistent with his general view of development. As children learn more about the world by having more social encounters, they become less egocentric. As they learn what communication is, egocentric speech loses any relevance it may have had for them. It simply fades away. The challenge facing Vygotsky was whether he could offer a credible alternative account of the disappearance of egocentric speech. If egocentric speech is so useful, why don't we all, adults and children, use it all the time?

In the course of Chapter 2 of *Thought and Language*, Vygotsky's answer to this question blossoms into a provocative theory of the development of the psychological conditions that give the term 'thinking for oneself' a meaning. For Piaget (1959), the main issue in development is how children come to leave an autistic or egocentric chamber of self-referential imagination or speech to become social participants who are in tune with reality. But for Vygotsky (1986), the main issue is how we ever come to develop the private space of self-consciousness that, as adults, we are used to inhabiting when we think. How, in other words, does thought come to be something that can be accomplished quietly, internally and for ourselves alone? Where Piaget asks how the door is opened on the privacy of the mind, Vygotsky asks how the room is built.

In Vygotsky's view, most children's primary experiences are not experiences of autistic isolation. Babies are typically surrounded by a rich cultural environment from the start. It would be very hard indeed for most babies to avoid this aspect of their environment because great efforts are typically undertaken by carers to involve them in that culture. As well as keeping babies warm, fed and comfortable, carers saturate babies' experience with speech, song and rhyme. Children's development of language use is, among other things, a matter of them figuring out and getting practice in all the different tasks that language can be used for. They get to practise in linguistic environments that are structured, sometimes deliberately and sometimes unwittingly, by the adults and older children around them. Their increasing linguistic competence is marked by an increasing discrimination in practice between different ways of using language. What different ways of using language are there?

Children can certainly gain adults' attention by crying. But with speech they can hold attention for longer. You may have had the experience of being continually asked 'why?' by a small child. Perhaps this repetitive questioning is driven by an insatiable curiosity. But perhaps it also reflects children's fascination that they can gain and hold adults' attention without first having to be hungry, in pain or uncomfortable. Asking 'why?' is a piece of small-scale social engineering. It patterns interaction and stabilizes it around the recognition that children are more than just bodies, that they are also social participants. Thus, children can use language to establish social presence much in the way that an adult asking another for a justification of a decision or an account of their behaviour might.

What is the value for a child of having a favourite colour and telling people about it? In some social and economic contexts a favourite colour might inform the selection and purchase of clothes and toys for the child. But, more fundamentally than this, the expression of a preference once again establishes the child as a social participant, as a person who has more about them than their physical body. When the favourite colour is known, this personhood can be elaborated on and given physical substance by the purchase of goods. Does the 'favouriteness' of the colour reflect some innate, unaccountable and previously unspoken sympathy between the child and a particular wavelength of light? Perhaps it does. Perhaps a child's communication of their favourite colour is just a simple transfer of information from one mind to another through the transparent medium of language. But, to elaborate from Vygotsky's (1986) position, it is more likely that 'favouriteness' is the outcome of a process in which someone invites the child into the condition of personhood by enquiring about their favourite. This might well occur when a child is rehearsing colour names with the help of a carer or older child.

In each of the uses of language I have considered so far, the 'communication' involved is not a simple matter of one mind transferring information to another through the transparent medium of language. Instead language got 'inside' the child. In the interactions I described, speech helped define what children are capable of socially and gave them ways to think about themselves. Speech can, of course, also be used to communicate needs and preferences from mind to mind, as it were. But it is also involved in building the private room that we call 'mind'. Vygotsky (1986) made this clear by setting children problems and watching how they went about solving them. For him, the reason egocentric speech use declines with age is that the 'talking to oneself' aspect of problem solving is gradually silenced as we become more practised in the use of the technology of language and as we encounter fewer novel problems. As language use is routinized, egocentric speech is first reduced to a whisper, then to sub-vocalization. A point can be reached at which nothing need be said for thought to take place. Thought can be silent as long as no novel problems present themselves. When they do, even adults will talk themselves through.

Conclusion

For Piaget (1927, 1959), cognitive development is based on the elaboration of the fundamental understanding that one is distinct from and separate within the rest of the world. In his distinctive account of children's cognitive and linguistic development, Vygotsky (1986) rejects Piaget's emphasis on separateness. This does not, however, lead Vygotsky to a position that rejects the possibility of 'thinking for oneself'. Rather, he argues that the growing child first becomes part of a language-using community, then, over time, as their cognitions become increasingly structured by language and as they become more practised in its use, the common property of language is gradually transformed into the silent, personal property of thought. Vygotsky's views on 'thinking for oneself' suggest that our understanding of this activity need not be limited to assumptions about the special capabilities of individual adults, but can instead be analysed through separability.

8 Norbert Elias
Being responsible for oneself

Introduction

The present section focuses on the themes of 'thinking for oneself' and 'being responsible for oneself'. As I argued in the previous chapter, these two highly valued aspects of independence are rarely seen as being in need of explanation. When account is made of them, they are understood to arise as part of a process of individual development that is fundamentally oriented toward separation from others, from their instructions and opinions. They are taken to be the property of well-developed adults and thus not the property of children. In this section, I have given myself the task of building alternative accounts of thinking for oneself and being responsible for oneself, accounts that rest on separability rather than on separation. I have two reasons for doing this.

The first reason is my sense that independence of mind and the capacity to take charge of oneself are often 'mystified'. They are treated as properties of the well-developed adult, properties that are held in independence of any other person. For example, if another helps you think for yourself, you cannot be thinking 'for yourself'. Likewise, no-one else can be held responsible for the quality of your self-responsibility. On its own, this independence would not necessarily be problematic, but there is a certain circularity at work in the way that these ideas support each other. Thinking for oneself and being responsible for oneself are properties that depend on independence, but in order for that independence to be respected as safe, appropriate and legitimate, it must be backed up by the ability to think for and take responsibility for oneself. When treated as the properties of individuals, then, thinking for oneself, being responsible for oneself and independence relate to each other as if they were a troupe of three acrobats, each one of whom tries to stand on another's shoulders, none of whom wishes to touch the floor. For us to think of an individual as embodying and possessing independence of mind or responsibility for self as personal qualities requires us systematically to ignore this circularity and to allow our impression of that individual to float unsupported, untroubled by the gravity of logic. There is a name for this mystification. It is called 'trust'. We can often trust another's judgement or trust them to be trustworthy. There are many circumstances, of course, where trust is tested against ground that seems more solid. Individuals, for example, acquire reputations. But children, as a class opposed to adults, are rarely trusted. How could they be trusted if the 'anti-gravity' of trust depends on the assumption of independence?

It is not my intention here to portray all trust as a delusion, mistake or logical error, rather to point out that it is distributed on the basis of a mystification. A person's 'good standing' in any social interaction that requires trust is treated as if it rested on the qualities they possess as an individual rather than being understood as itself generated through social processes. This mystification, though it is necessary for many forms of social interaction, does children no favours when their interests, views and accounts come into conflict with those of the adults who surround them. Why not, then, abandon the themes of thinking for and being responsible for oneself entirely as if they were nothing more than ideological constructs that maintain illegitimate inequalities? This question opens up my second reason for trying to reimagine these themes. Although I am suspicious of the mystification of these properties of independence, I do not think children, or anyone else, would benefit from the outright abandonment of these tokens of human value. Put simply, being able to decide, against prevailing opinion, that a state of affairs is wrong or is doing you harm, and then having the courage to try to change that state of affairs is of inestimable value to people of any age who are experiencing physical or psychological oppression. I want to conserve these human capacities, and I want to understand them better. What interests me is the sense of how that ability and that courage do not depend on a set of properties that we can take for granted as belonging to individuals, but are instead collective achievements.

In the previous chapter, I argued that Vygotsky (1986) gave us an account of the privacy of cognition, the fact that we feel our thoughts as our own and can think for ourselves, as a result of our introduction to and growing familiarity with the collectively owned, maintained and developed 'institution' of spoken language. If Vygotsky is right, then the walls that establish the privacy of thought are built of collective property. Given this, it makes more sense to see independence of mind as a patterning of separability than as the result of a process of separation. If we take this view, then those more controversial aspects of 'children's rights' that would require adults to respect children's points of view, in other words, to trust them on occasion, would not appear to be the imposition of an artificial expectation on those too 'naturally' incompetent to have minds of their own. It would instead be understood as the repetition and elaboration of an ancient human activity, as old as spoken language, in which collectively owned institutions create fresh competences in human relations by altering patterns of separability. Persons taking an institutional rather than an individual view of the conditions underlying trust, are likely to be at once less mystified by it and less frightened of the monstrous 'child with rights'.

Having argued in the previous chapter for the place of separability in 'thinking for oneself', I now turn to matters of responsibility for oneself. What could be more private and less open to coherent analysis than a moral relationship that one has with oneself and oneself alone? As in the previous chapter, my aim is to give a fresh account of a seemingly private and individual property, an account that demystifies that property by asking how it is built and what it is made of. I am going to tell a story about self-control and trustworthiness through a reading of some of Elias's work on what he calls the 'civilizing process' (Elias 1994). The story will begin with the human body and with questions of the separation between or separability of the human body and the social person. At first glance, this might look like a false start. How can bodies and responsibility be related in any way? After all, bodies are physical objects and responsibility is social or moral, it is about meanings, not things. The connection is to be found in the role that bodies have long had in the establishment of hierarchies of status and power and in the establishment of relationships of belonging. In Chapter 2, I suggested that in the establishment of 'racial' hierarchies, the further a race could be understood to have 'evolved' away from a natural state of savagery, closely associated with skin tone, the better for that 'race'. In Chapter 6, I argued that transitional phenomena allow children and carers to establish basic assumptions of belonging. Because the child is a body, but is also more than a body, she can own herself as well as be owned by her carers and, on that basis, can begin to belong to the social and symbolic, as well as to the physical and natural. In both cases bodies take the role of symbols with implications for status and belonging.

In the present chapter I will argue that Elias's (1994) work on manners and etiquette relates embodiment, responsibility and status through an historical examination of self-control, or the muting of natural drives. I will further argue that what Elias calls 'muting' might equally be termed 'concealment'. To look like one is in control of and therefore responsible for oneself requires the formation of a backstage area of social space in which it is safe to do things that would otherwise look 'out of control'. I will argue that this backstage space is, somewhat paradoxically, marked out by social processes as lying outside the social, that manners and etiquette involve the concealment in full view of our animality and embodiment. For those of us who are 'civilized' in Elias's sense, social space always has a pocket we can put our natures in and this pocket depends on separability. Crucially, these features of 'civilization' emerged as European societies made the transition from feudalism to individualized modernity. First, however, I need to give a broader introduction to Elias and to his project.

Elias, civilization and the barbaric

Elias's major work *The Civilising Process* was originally published in German in 1939. The book is divided into two sections. In my discussion of his work I will draw mainly on section one, entitled 'The History of Manners' which focuses on the control of physiological drives such as eating and excreting. Section two, 'State Formation and Civilization', focuses on the control of force and violence. Elias begins his preface to the book with a brief discussion of the difference between the 'barbaric' and the 'civilized' (Elias 1994: ix). So, my first task in introducing him is to clarify his use of these two terms.

A journalist once asked Mahatma Ghandi, the great campaigner against British imperial rule of the Indian sub-continent, what he thought of Western civilization. Ghandi replied that he thought it would be a good idea. Considering that his mother was killed in a Nazi concentration camp, I can imagine Elias echoing the sentiment. It is not Elias's (1994) aim to establish the superiority of Western culture over other cultures, or Westerners over other people. But, rather like Bernstein (1971) on language and class (see Chapter 3), he does ask us to consider differences between societies and people's perceptions of those differences. He suggests that: 'If members of present-day Western civilized society were to find themselves suddenly transported into a past epoch of their own society, such as the medieval-feudal period, they would find there much that they esteem "uncivilized" in other societies today' (Elias 1994: ix). By saying this, Elias is suggesting that the term 'civilized', whatever other connotations it has, does indicate a set of recognizable differences between societies. The task he then sets himself is to elucidate what it means for a society's members to consider themselves 'civilized' and to describe the processes by which European medieval-feudal societies became 'civilized'. Norbert Elias was a sociologist. Consequently he was committed to explaining recognizable differences between societies in terms of how those societies are organized rather than in terms of the innate qualities of the persons who belong to them. Thus, while he clearly deals with the same topics as a Western supremacist might, his strategy runs counter to the main trends of racist imperialist thought.

For Elias, civilized societies are organized in such a way that the right to use physical force or violence to settle disputes or to enforce one's will is monopolized by the state and its agents. Thus, while a soldier at war on behalf of the state may be encouraged to kill, for a civilian to slap a fellow customer's face in a dispute at a supermarket checkout is a criminal offence. Civilized societies are characterized by the attempt to drain force and violence from everyday life by deploying a distinction between the legitimate and illegitimate use of force. Whenever police officers arrest someone for assaulting another, it may appear that they are acting on behalf of the victim. But in a civilized society that has a public police force rather than private guards for hire, these matters are rather less personal. If police were to act directly on behalf of the victim, this would be a corrupt side-effect of a much more abstract relationship. Police do not act on behalf of specific victims of crime but on behalf of the state. Violent conduct is discouraged by policing, prosecution and imprisonment so as to reinforce and continually remake the distinction between legitimate and illegitimate violence. This serves the end of keeping the ambient level of violence in society relatively low. Ideally, then, policing is impartial, preferring no individual over any other, because police owe their allegiance not to any individual but to the state and to the maintenance of the legitimate/illegitimate distinction.

According to Elias (1994), this state of affairs has consequences for the attitudes individuals hold about their own emotions. If violent conflict must be avoided, so must florid displays of anger. In a civilized society to 'lose your temper' can be shaming, and civilized people have learned strategies of self-constraint that prevent them from bringing shame upon themselves. Hot tempers often receive a cool response. Think of the politeness with which a well-trained service sector employee will try to manage an unruly customer. The contrast Elias wants us to recognize is between feudal and contemporary European societies, between the Middle Ages and modernity. Before there were police and national armed forces, there were bands of soldiers, loyal to and paid by private individuals. Before losing your temper became shameful, displays of fury were something to be proud of, as long as you could win any subsequent test of strength. Being civilized means, in part, living with the obligation to constrain one's own emotions and conduct. The idea of the obligation to self-constraint may sound familiar. Elias was strongly influenced by Freud's (1962) account of taboo and the origins of civilization that I examined in Chapter 2. Elias's (1994) work can be considered an attempt to give Freud's near mythical account of possible pre-historic processes some real historical referents. For Elias, as for Freud, there is more to civilization than the distribution of violence. There are also the matters of bodies, manners and disgust.

Table manners

In the eleventh century a Venetian doge married a Greek princess. In her Byzantine circle the fork was clearly in use. At any rate, we hear that she lifted food to her mouth 'by means of little golden forks with two prongs'. This gave rise in Venice to a dreadful scandal: 'This novelty was regarded as so excessive a sign of refinement that the dogaressa was severely rebuked by the ecclesiastics who called down divine wrath upon her. Shortly afterward she was afflicted by a repulsive illness and St Bonaventure did not hesitate to declare that this was a punishment of God.'

(Elias 1994: 59)

While many contemporary readers will find the use of a fork at table not only unremarkable but also practical and hygienic, religious authorities of the eleventh century called down a curse on this woman for using one. They may, of course, have had political motivations and may have wanted to embarrass the dogaressa or, indirectly, the doge. But what was it about the use of the fork that gave them their opportunity?

At that time in Venice, the 'standard eating technique' (Elias 1994: 58) had no place for the fork but it had certain other key features.

> In the houses of the more wealthy, the platters are usually taken from the sideboard ... Everyone takes – or sends for – what he fancies at the moment. People help themselves from communal dishes. Solids (above all, meat) are taken by hand, liquids with ladles or spoons. But soups and sauces are still very frequently drunk. Plates and dishes are lifted to the mouth. For a long period too, there are no special implements for different foods. The same knife or spoon is used. The same glasses are drunk from. Frequently two diners eat from the same board.
>
> (1994: 58)

According to Elias, this standard medieval eating technique was not the result of a simple absence of manners or civility. Rather it was a solution to the problem of distributing food that incorporated and respected a particular set of feelings about how people should relate to each other. The dogaressa's fork offended these feelings. Indications that the standard, communal arrangement was not random are to be found in the caution that diners had to exercise to ensure that those of higher social rank started eating before others (1994: 58). Elias elaborates thus: 'People who ate together in the way customary in the Middle Ages, taking meat with their fingers from the same dish, wine from the same goblet, soup from the same pot or same plate ... such people stood in a different relationship to one another than we do' (1994: 60). In these relationships, the business of marking out and respecting separation between individuals was far less important than marking out and respecting social rank. Though Elias's detailed historical evidence reveals a far more complex and various process of change between feudal and contemporary societies, his views on the shifting ways in which value is distributed bear comparison with Taylor's (Taylor and Gutmann 1992) as discussed in Chapter 2. Since they were not organized by the principle of the discrete individual, medieval table manners showed no evidence of '[the] invisible wall of affects, which now seems to rise between one human body and another, repelling and separating, the wall which is often perceptible today at the mere approach of something that has been in contact with the mouth or hands of someone else' (Elias 1994: 60).

Natural functions and etiquette

So far, Elias's (1994) work indicates that if we are interested in issues of separation, self-control and responsibility, the field of manners and etiquette may repay our attention. With Elias's help I have been able to suggest that there are links between separateness, status and some apparently trivial matters of everyday conduct. I have yet to focus, as promised above, on the body. Fortunately, Elias builds his argument by drawing on a survey of books of etiquette dating from the thirteenth to the twentieth century, much of which concerns such topics as urination, spitting and farting. Over the next few sections I will use this material to sketch the development of civilized conduct, of disgust and of concealment.

Advice on defecation and urination

> It is impolite to greet someone who is urinating or defecating.
>
> (Elias 1994: 110)

Consider the quotation above that Elias drew from a handbook of etiquette dating from 1530. From a modern perspective, it is remarkable that this advice should appear in a handbook of etiquette at all. Surely it is the height of bad manners for an author to refer to such topics so directly and thus risk offending or embarrassing his readers? So what is an author on etiquette doing using these words? The second odd thing about it is its content. To many contemporary readers it would simply go without saying that one should not greet someone who is urinating or defecating. This for the simple reason that the majority of acts of excretion take place after people have already hidden themselves away, using the architecture of the modern toilet, a bush or another makeshift screen to absent themselves from social intercourse. The opportunity to meet someone face-to-face in the middle of their business is a rare one indeed. If someone has not attempted to hide themselves, many of us would interpret that as a sign of derangement or drunkenness making it very unlikely that we would hail them. Further, many of us find excretion so embarrassing that not only do we spontaneously hide ourselves away, but we will also hide the fact that we are hiding by deploying euphemisms to excuse ourselves from company. If one is attempting to pass as a civilized person, one is well advised to say 'excuse me for a moment' rather than 'I am going for a poo'. The quotation clearly refers to a world in which acts of excretion were not hidden by everybody. It advises readers to erect an imaginary screen to 'hide' anyone who has not hidden themselves away. As Elias argues, Erasmus, the author of the quotation, was advancing the threshold of embarrassment, shame and repugnance around the signs of bodily nature. But he was writing at a time before it had become embarrassing to acknowledge and openly to discuss means of concealing bodily nature. By 1774 some authors had begun to conceal concealment itself, deploying circumlocutions and making a rule of silence about bodily functions:

> as far as natural needs are concerned, it is proper (even for children) to satisfy them where one cannot be seen. It is never proper to speak of the parts of the body that should always be hidden, or of certain bodily necessities to which nature has subjected us, or even to mention them.
>
> (Elias 1994: 113)

From this small example, it is clear that, on Elias's view, becoming civilized involved the formation of a peculiar new relationship between persons and their 'bodily necessities'. Subjected to these necessities by nature, it becomes the civilized person's obligation to conceal this relationship with nature and further, to efface, forget and erase the memory of the concealment. This operation, carried out with the help of, among other things, architecture, plumbing, predictable patterns of feeling and the discretion of others, converts phenomena that are outside one's control into phenomena that can be treated as if they were naturally and automatically separate from the rest of one's life. Shitting is treated as if it were something that could itself successfully be shat out.

The practice of concealing concealment is an attempt to turn the effort of hiding our subjection to nature into apparently effortless second nature. It helps us mark ourselves out as individuals independent of our animality, to live, for example, as if food were a lifestyle choice replaceable by fresh air if necessary. Such is the significance of trying to make excretion invisible. Of course, since we are bodies, it is impossible for us to actually and completely separate ourselves in this way, but if we want to pass as civilized beings, we can still perform separateness against a backdrop of separability. In this matter, the flexible nature of sociality is of vital importance. If confronted by someone defecating in the street, we may or may not acknowledge their existence. We can ignore them and avoid commenting on them to our companions. Thus we can alter the pattern of separability in our relationship with the offending sight, so as to partially and temporarily separate ourselves from it and from our own natures. Similarly, if our own bodies threaten to reveal our connections with animality by signalling a need to excrete, we can seek refuge in a private space and thereby maintain the appearance of separateness. At this point it is worth noting that ever since the early days of this civilizing process, the failure to conceal and to conceal concealment has been associated with low status persons, as this quote from 1570 illustrates:

> One should not like rustics who have not been to court or lived among refined and honourable people, relieve oneself without shame or reserve in front of ladies, or before the doors or windows of court chambers or other rooms.
>
> (Elias 1994: 111)

Advice on blowing one's nose

> Thirteenth century: 'Precept for gentlemen . . . When you blow your nose or cough, turn round so that nothing falls on the table.'
>
> (Elias 1994: 121)

For Elias, the history of the handkerchief parallels that of the fork. In the Middle Ages, bare hands were good enough for picking up food and for blowing one's nose. As time went by, practices of separation and concealment became more important. In the thirteenth century it was important that mucus did not fall on the table, but no attempt was made to hide the sneezing face. By the sixteenth century, the handkerchief was enabling the concealment of mucus, its use linked to the presence or absence of important people, thus: 'it is proper to wipe the nostrils with a handkerchief, and to do this while turning away, if more honourable people are present' (Elias 1994: 122). Soon, the concealment of the concealment of the mucus became vital to good conduct. Consider the following quotations:

> Nor is it seemly, after wiping your nose, to spread out your handkerchief and peer into it as if pearls and rubies might have fallen out of your head.
>
> (Elias 1994: 123)

> to blow your nose openly into your handkerchief, without concealing yourself with your serviette, and to wipe away your sweat with it . . . are filthy habits.
>
> (Elias 1994: 124)

> You should always use your handkerchief to blow your nose ... and
> in doing so usually hide your face with your hat.
>
> (Elias 1994: 124)

Once again, tools and techniques, coupled with the complicity of one's
companions, allow the civilized person to live as if separate from their bodily
nature which can safely be folded away and stored in a pocket for later attention or disposal. When the body announces its presence like a barnyard
animal, civilized persons conspire to pretend that nothing has happened.
Hand in hand with the spreading tendency to practise the concealment of
concealment runs a tendency to ignore the pleasurable aspects of inhabiting a
defecating, urinating, sneezing body and to emphasize its disgusting side, its
dirt and inconvenience. Polite company does not entertain reports of a satisfying bowel evacuation, nor does it celebrate the pleasures of desperately
needed urinary relief. Pearls and rubies do not tumble from our noses, but
why should we not be curious about what does? This civilized editing of
experience is reflected in the fate of another potentially satisfying but more
voluntary activity – spitting.

Advice on spitting

As with the earlier examples, a clear arc of spitting manners can be plotted
through the centuries. We begin in feudal society where human value is
distributed according to proximity to the monarch. In such societies spitting
is managed through only the simplest courtesies, and there is little anxiety
about being seen spitting: 'Do not spit over or on the table ... Do not spit into
the bowl when washing your hands' (Elias 1994: 129). By the sixteenth century, the courtesy of turning away to avoid spitting on others begins to carry
overtones of concealment, where the foot and the handkerchief cover purulent sputum: 'Turn away when spitting, lest your saliva fall on someone. If
anything purulent falls to the ground, it should be trodden upon, lest it
nauseate someone. If you are not at liberty to do this, catch the sputum in a
small cloth' (Elias 1994: 130). As we reach the eighteenth century not only
must spit be concealed, but the concealing of spit must itself be concealed:

> After spitting into your handkerchief, you should fold it at once,
> without looking at it, and put it into your pocket. You should take
> great care never to spit on your clothes or those of others ... If you
> notice saliva on the ground, you should immediately put your foot
> adroitly on it. If you notice any on someone's coat, it is not polite to
> make it known; you should instruct a servant to remove it. If no
> servant is present, you should remove it yourself without being

noticed. For good breeding consists in not bringing to people's attention anything that might offend or confuse them.

(Elias 1994: 131)

Discussion

So far, Elias's (1994) work has shown us that, over time, European societies' treatment of natural functions changed. Where once it had simply been a matter of courtesy to shield others, especially those of a higher status, from the direct effects of one's involuntary bodily functions, these functions were to become shrouded in shame and experienced as disgusting. By the eighteenth century not only should a 'civilized' person try to conceal those functions, but they should also attempt to conceal their acts of concealment. For example, not only should one blow one's nose into a handkerchief rather than on the floor, but further, one should turn away from company while doing so, or hide behind one's hat. The quicker the unwanted produce of an uncontrolled bodily function could be packaged and pocketed, the better. As you might already have had occasion to remark, not all contemporary Europeans observe the requirements of civilized conduct. Elias's (1994) argument is not troubled by this observation since he is well aware that these systems of manners are also systems of social exclusion. 'Rustics' and others who lack honour or breeding are continually posited as the opposite of the well-mannered person. Though social elites of one form or another are a constant of European societies, the basis on which the elite is formed changes over time. For Elias, it is these changes in the way human value is distributed that account for changes in manners from the merely courteous to the repressively civilized. As I suggested above, the key transition is from feudal court-based society where one's value was based on proximity to the monarch, to a modern individualized society in which one's value depends on one's ability to maintain the impression of separateness. The multiple, double-layered concealments of otherwise uncontrollable bodily functions that come to define civilized conduct are effective markers of distance between the individual and nature. They help to build the invisible walls between individuals that interest Elias so much by concealing what makes us the same as all other human animals and thus highlighting our individuality as social persons.

By this point it should be clear just what peculiar and particular performances are involved in establishing one's good standing in a civilized individualized society. In order to remain within one's boundary and be recognized as a person in good standing, one must control what one can of one's animality and one must hide what one cannot control. If one cannot demonstrate dominion over one's own body, what claim can one have on being more than a body? Social being depends on performing separation from others and from one's body. Only those who control or conceal the disgusting parts of themselves are to be accepted and trusted with further responsibilities. To be trusted at this most basic level, one must also be complicit with others, helping them to conceal and to ignore their bodies. Thus, responsible people, those who are not rude, crude, silly or vulgar help each other to hide human embodiment in full view. While these performances make one look independent, the performance is only possible through dependency on the tools and learned techniques of concealment. Social individuals momentarily separate themselves from their mucus, only to return it in hidden form to their own pockets.

Conclusion

This chapter is focussed on a question: What is 'responsibility' made of and how is it built? Obviously the scope of the topic 'responsibility' exceeds the terms of reference I have used here. Nevertheless, by tracing the origins of civilized concealments, Elias (1994) gives us reason to link good social standing in contemporary society (being seen as trustworthy) with a collectively built and maintained informal institution for the distribution of human value. In the matter of appearing responsible, a familiarity with tools and techniques of bodily concealment precedes any interior personal quality. For example, in all other ways an individual may be an excellent candidate for a job, but if they yawn, belch, sneeze or fart in the interview and make no attempt at concealment, they are unlikely to succeed. Would it improve their position if they were to apologize? Perhaps it would, but in view of what Elias has shown us about concealment, to talk openly about such a loss of control is almost as embarrassing as the 'belch' itself. To fail to conceal and to conceal the concealment is to announce oneself as irresponsible. It shows that one is unwilling or unable to conspire in the collective, civilized business of separating ourselves from our bodies and from each other. It is offensive because it damages everyone's identity.

Throughout his book Elias draws attention to resemblances between the 'uncivilized' and children. In this he sometimes risks self-contradiction. He points out that a member of a feudal court, though generally unconcerned with concealment, nevertheless holds to a code of conduct, 'courtesy' (1994: 87), that matches and supports the pattern of courtly social relationships. To equate this with the situation of a young child who has yet to find his feet in public life of any kind would be wrong. Nevertheless, among his other achievements, Elias has demystified the matter of responsibility by showing us what it is made of. Tools and techniques for upholding separateness from each other and from our own bodies must be learnt by any child who wants to be trusted. The simple fact that children are learning these tools and techniques makes adults less inclined to trust them and to see them as capable of bearing responsibility. Elias's (1994) work, then, leaves me with a question. Many children are less able to conspire in the business of pretending that we are separate from our bodies and from each other than many adults. This, I have argued, lies at the heart of the tendency to trust adults over children. But is this a sound basis for excluding them from participating in making decisions that affect them?

PART 5
HUMAN VALUE AND CHILDHOOD

In Parts 1 and 2, I argued that resistance to the concept of children's rights in otherwise modern and individualistic cultures grows out of an association between high social status and the performance of 'separateness'. I argued that the more one is able to foreground one's independence from other people and one's distance from 'nature' and the historical and personal past, the more respect one can expect to be given. Naturally, people who successfully perform separateness are still able to acknowledge family or colleagues, but in the status performances that are a focal point of their identity, the impression is given that the individual's success could have been reached by any route, thus that the involvement of particular others was merely accidental. In Chapter 2, I illustrated how this association informed major lines of division among human beings in the nineteenth century, making racism, sexism and ageism appear legitimate. In Chapters 3 and 4, I argued that the link between status and separation has persisted into the twentieth century. It was certainly reflected in the differences between working- and middle-class culture in mid-twentieth-century England and, as working-class solidarity is becoming a less widespread feature of European life, is extending its franchise among fresh segments of the population. Throughout these chapters I argued that a fixation on separateness skews understandings of the idea of children's rights, especially their rights of participation, so that the adjustment to patterns of separability it offers are systematically misunderstood as providing the conditions for the growth of monstrous children who will know and accept no love, no authority, no guidance and no restraint.

The main aim of this book is to give conceptual form to the hope that love and rights can co-exist in children's lives by elaborating the concept of separability. Part 1 concentrated on interpreting the Convention, a legal instrument. So by Part 3, I was anxious that separability not be understood as a solely legal phenomenon. I wanted to show that separability is just as significant in informal settings. So I gave more intimate and developmental substance to the concept, drawing on Gilligan (1982) and Winnicott (1971).

In their work I found lively and flexible understandings of human value that are rooted in an appreciation of separability rather than a fixation on separateness. I also found indications that, though one can never be separate from one's body, entry into social life and into the possibility of self-possession involves entry into a broad arena of separability by way of transitional objects.

When adults consider children's rights, they are often concerned that children lack the necessary competences to use them constructively. Though I would argue that this response arises from a fixation on separateness that excludes the possibility that children might be assisted in the use of their rights, I still felt a need to address this concern head on. So in Part 4, I chose to examine two tokens of competence, the abilities to think for oneself and to take responsibility for oneself. With the help of Vygotsky (1986) and Elias (1994), I argued that these tokens of competence are collective achievements rather than individual properties. I further argued that they were best understood as elements of human institutions, such as spoken language and manners, that help us distribute separabilities in our own lives and experience, and thereby render us 'competent'. Taking this view of competence it is much easier to see children's rights as described in the Convention as an institution that distributes separabilities, an institution with the potential to refresh human competences in the matter of relationships between adults and children.

This is the final section of the book. In Chapter 10, I will conclude by summarizing my argument through three themes. First, however, there is more to say about separability. Throughout the book I have argued that, despite the equalizing potential of individualism, ascriptions of value still tend to be based on hierarchies of separation. Thus, in its various guises, the idea of level of development has often functioned as a 'field-guide to people', enabling rapid and certain evaluation. I have asserted separability as prior to separation so as to destabilize the hierarchical relationships between adults and children that the idea of level of development allows for. All hierarchies of value that are based on separation are similarly vulnerable. For example, once it was recognized that in reality 'white' people are no further advanced, no further from nature than any other 'racial' group, then treating black people as possessions and as mere objects became abhorrent. Likewise, once it was recognized that even though many women can give birth, they do not have closer ties with 'nature' than men, then it became clear that to deny women full opportunities to participate in society would be to underestimate their value as human individuals. Thus, each particular racist, sexist or ageist hierarchy of value can safely be tackled one at a time in the name of an equality of value that rests on the assertion that each human deserves the same level of respect as every other. But what of the value of humanity itself? What happens to the basic value that we might want to ascribe equally to every human being regardless of ethnicity, gender or age when separability replaces separation in our understanding of value?

As long as the distribution of human value was based on separation, some people were more likely to be seen as closer to nature than others and these same people were more likely to be treated as 'things', lacking voice, identity and significance for their own sake. Such people might find themselves treated as possessions and used for others' purposes, regardless of their own wishes. Extreme as such a situation is, plenty of men, women and children have faced it throughout history, and many still face it today. To challenge separation as a basis for distributing human value is to challenge the legitimacy of social arrangements in which human beings are treated as if they were beasts or things. But if we are consistent in our application of separability, a rather surprising possibility arises. The very idea that humanity itself has value is grounded on two separations. The separation of culture from nature ensures that we can think of ourselves as more than animals. The separation of the social person from matter ensures that we can think of ourselves as more than our bodies, more than things. Thus separation has not only grounded discriminations among humans that we might want to resist, but it has also grounded discriminations between humans and everything else that there is. This has given us the sense that we humans are special and especially valuable. The separation of humans from beasts and from things is both the foundation and moral substance of human rights. Of course, there are many people who would wish to expand that sense of value beyond the borders of our own species, and there are faiths that insist on the value of all living things. There are even a few sociologists (Latour 1993) who urge us to reconsider the value of material objects. But specifically human value appears to be based on two excluding separations. Given this, is it the case that a consistent assertion of separability over separation will not only dissolve discrimination among humans, but will also corrode belief in human value itself?

In the following chapter I will address this difficult issue. I have chosen to do so with the help of Deleuze and Guattari (1983, 1988), respectively a philosopher and a psychiatrist. As we shall see, their shared interests covered many areas, but they consistently have addressed questions of organization and value with concepts comparable to separability.

9 Deleuze and Guattari
Separability and the composition of human value

Introduction

During the social and political ferment of Paris in the late 1960s, the attention of a number of French intellectuals was drawn to an earlier time of revolution. The French Revolution of 1789 overthrew the existing monarchy. The revolutionaries marched under the slogan 'Liberty, fraternity, equality'. The revolution was an example of the deployment of the idea that each and every person is of equal value. It was one of the political pinnacles of a broad cultural and intellectual movement called the 'Enlightenment'. Though Christian tradition had long allowed that all people are equal in the eyes of God, the enlightened view was that all people should be considered fundamentally equal in each other's eyes. In other words, the Enlightenment insisted that humans recognize their own value, a value that is rooted in their humanity, and thus ascribe equal value to each other by virtue of this common identity. So it was that the plantation slaves of Haiti in the Caribbean staged their own revolution in 1804, equally fired by enlightened self and mutual respect as the French. So it was that the French and American Republics came to recognize each other as comrades in a common struggle for human dignity against religious and royal oppression. As the philosopher Kant would argue (1983), enlightenment was nothing more complicated than a recognition of something that had always been with us, our human powers of rational thought. All we had to do was wake up to the truth of who we had always been, a truth that had been concealed from us by a combination of political oppression and our own intellectual idleness. Once we recognized our capacities for reasoned, independent thought, we could then establish our independence and determine the shape of our own lives.

By the 1960s, however, certain contradictions of enlightened society had become quite apparent. On the one hand, enlightenment meant self-determination for all human beings in virtue of their humanity. On the other hand, many enlightened practices still involved denying the dignity of self-determination to certain key groups who were understood to lack the reasoning powers that would separate them from the natural world. Under enlightenment, for example, children and the mentally ill (Foucault 1971) become subject to intervention and control designed by the rational to protect them from themselves. For such authors as Foucault (1971) and De-leuze and Guattari (1983, 1988), it became axiomatic that enlightenment was not the simple discovery of a hitherto concealed common, rational human character, but was instead a process of social change in which those who were already powerless enough to be found wanting were decisively marked off as being in need of instruction, cure or schooling. It was this separation itself that shored up the idea of a common rational human character that all could develop toward, an idea that otherwise had no empirical foundation. For these authors, the human sciences that I examined in Chapter 2, concerned as they were with 'development', were a major contributory factor in the establishment and elaboration of a distinctively enlightened pattern of social control. As a result of their views, these authors are sometimes collectively, and crudely, described as 'anti-enlightenment' or as 'anti-humanist'. A less prejudicial term to indicate this approach to human value is 'post-structural'.

In this chapter I will argue that post-structural insights into the en-lightened idea of common humanity do not necessarily entail a rejection of such concepts as 'human rights'. But if we take these insights into account, we will be unwilling to base our understandings of politics, culture, and ulti-mately human value on the, now compromised, developmental horizon of a common, rational human character. At first glance this would appear to threaten the value we place on each and every individual human being. If the foundation of enlightened discourse is put in question, there is no longer a compelling reason to assume that there is a single property called 'humanity' that can decisively distinguish us from beasts and from things. This would leave human rights without foundation. In this chapter, however, I will argue that Deleuze and Guattari (1983, 1988) are not in the business of destroying all and any sense of human value. Instead, whilst they do not accept the enlightened equation of humanity with rationality, they do offer us a fresh way of understanding human value. For them, human value is not to be discovered, as Kant (1983) had it, but is always to be built. Human value is not a single hidden treasure, but is the diverse and changing consequence of processes of organization and re-organization. Deleuze and Guattari (1983, 1988) forged a number of concepts that help clarify this position. Each of their key concepts, as we shall see, is already 'immunized' against any prior assumption of human distinctiveness. The first such concept that I will consider is 'territorialization' (Deleuze and Guattari 1983: 296).

Territorialization

In Chapter 4, I gave an account of the economic changes that led to the decline of honour as the key principle for the distribution of human value and the rise of dignity to replace it. This account contained a good example of territorialization. As you may recall, in monarchic or feudal society, the monarch was the focus and source of all the value that could be ascribed to persons. One's position in the hierarchy of honour depended principally on one's proximity by birth to the monarch. What made this distribution of value possible? Agriculture was the main economic activity of feudal society. Thus, ownership of land was key to economic and political power. There was always scope for interminable conflict over land ownership. By marking a monarch out as the notional owner of all land, while leaving effective control of that land much more widely distributed, potentially interminable conflict could be stilled. It is important to note here that the institution of the monarchy did not emerge as a result of one peaceful conference of rival powers in which they finally focused their powers of reason on the problem of discord. No doubt meetings did take place in which alliances were formed, alliances often sealed by the exchange of children in marriage. Even though many individuals and their plans and desires contributed to it, however, the overall process of the emergence of monarchy was not in the hands of any individual or group of individuals. If monarchy was a solution to a problem of organization, it was a solution that emerged through conflict and trial and under certain conditions, both human and non-human. As long as the economy was based on land, as long as the land was productive and as long as people were willing and able to fight each other for control of that land, monarchy was simply the most sustainable principle of organization. This means that at certain times under certain circumstances, monarchy was more effective at gathering and retaining available resources than rival forms of organization. Thus, as long as the conditions and relationships that led to the emergence of monarchy pertained, the institution of monarchy was continually reproduced. It is of central significance here that 'honour', a particular form of human value, was built from a patterning of elements that were not themselves exclusively human and that the pattern was not set by human decisions alone.

So far, I have outlined monarchy and its relation to honour. But what can the concept of territorialization contribute to our understanding of human value in this case? In feudal times, territory in the form of legitimate claim to the use of land, lay at the heart of value. Processes for the production of economic value were tightly tied into processes for the distribution of territory. Likewise, processes for the production of personal value were tightly tied into processes for the distribution of territory. In this quite simple sense then, honour, like the pattern of interacting elements that created and sustained it, was highly territorialized. This might seem to be no more than a literal description, one in which the word 'territory' gains a few syllables but little extra meaning. But there is more to the concept of territorialization than this. It is probably quite apparent that the emergence of honour was not an historical inevitability. It depended on a wide range of conditions that came together in just such a way as to give it wide currency and durability over time. It may be less apparent that there was no inevitability about the emergence of monarchy. Its emergence and its reproduction over time were dependent on many factors. For some time, this dependency was the source of its strength, but eventually it would become a source of weakness. This leads me on to the second of Deleuze and Guattari's (1983) concepts that concern us.

De-territorialization

'Trade' is the transfer and exchange of goods over distance. Even at the height of monarchies' territorialization of economic and human value, long-distance trade routes still functioned. In early times, available means of transport tended to restrict economically worthwhile trade to luxury goods, like spices, fabrics and precious minerals. This sort of trade played into the honour system and gave it symbolic elaboration and reinforcement, supplying, for example, the special costumes of honourable people. The length of the trade routes meant that even within a highly territorialized regime, there were people who either crossed territory themselves or made a living by processing extra-territorial raw materials. Thus, some small sectors of the mainly agrarian economy, such as long-distance trade in luxury goods and the crafts that processed them remained relatively de-territorialized, they existed 'marginally in the pores of this old social body' (Deleuze and Guattari 1983: 225). Over time, a number of factors allowed this de-territorialized sector to expand. First, monarchy had a tendency to cleanse areas of minor skirmishes over the ownership of land, thus reducing traders' risk of getting caught up in local conflict. Second, monarchies had an interest in gathering information about and communicating with each other. Trade routes were the principal medium for this flow of information and benefited from the sanction and protection of the powers of the lands they passed through. Third, as monarchic states began to compete with each other for economic and military power, they invested in shipping and exploration. This opened up new trade routes and increased the bulk of goods that could be transferred, making it economically worthwhile to trade in ever less precious raw materials. These factors helped to develop and to enrich the relatively de-territorialized segments of the population who would eventually transform the principle underlying the distribution of value from honour to dignity, from the value of connection and preservation to the value of separation and transformation.

Dignity, then, was born within a broad de-territorialization (Deleuze and Guattari 1983: 296) of the value of goods, human productive labour and persons. Though dignity was notionally available to all, the fate of the spirit of enlightenment makes it clear that it became attached to some persons more than it did to others. Once it had been generated as de-territorialized value, dignity was also re-territorialized onto 'self-made' individuals. There is a 'magic' of dignity that is a consequence of de-territorialization. Since many of the connections and relationships that gave the 'self-made' their wealth were highly distributed over the space of trade and the time of investment and thus not available for direct inspection, where dignity condensed out of the mist of reputation, it took the form of the independent individual who needed no support. Even though the dignified faced a wider range of risks to their wealth and status because of their widely distributed pattern of their dependencies, these dependencies were often hidden from consciousness. In contrast, the relatively stable grounds of honour – land and inheritance – had always been in clear view, thus giving a readily available account of a person's place within the hierarchy of honour. Deleuze and Guattari's (1983) account of the development of capitalism and of the 'separate' individual, gives us a further explanation of why otherwise de-territorialized dignity was, in practice, unequally distributed among individuals: 'on the one side, the de-territorialized worker who has become free and naked, having to sell his labour capacity; and on the other, decoded money that has become capital and is capable of buying it' (Deleuze and Guattari 1983: 225).

With the decline of monarchy it was always possible that dignity could belong to all and remain fully de-territorialized. But it so happened that just as personal value was de-territorialized, so was economic value. I have already noted that land ownership lost a great deal of its significance through de-territorialization. This was because it became just another of the many things that could be traded for money, with or without the agreement of a monarch. People's labour also became negotiable in this way. Once their labour power was detached from the land, it was open to being bought and sold for money. It was this coincidence of de-territorializations that allowed for the accumulation of capital by some at the expense of others, and, thus, for the development of inequalities of dignity. Owners of capital could lay claim to the fact of dignity, leaving only the dream of dignity for those who owned nothing but their labour.

In my illustration of Deleuze and Guattari's (1983) concepts so far, it should be clear that for them, as for Marx (Marx and Engels 1998) (see Chapter 4), the organization that distributes human value and the re-organization that redistributes it are not the result of the will or rational planning of any individual or group of individuals. Considered from Deleuze and Guattari's (1983) perspective, they are instead the result of complex co-incidences and synergies that, while they inevitably include individual human struggle and problem solving, are beyond human control. Deleuze and Guattari illustrate this with a list of conditions underlying the transformation of monarchic states into capitalist states. The age of capitalism is a period of time ... for the conjunction of all the decoded and de-territorialized flows ... an accumulation of property deeds – in land, for example – will be necessary in a first period of time, in a favourable conjuncture, at a time when this property costs little (the disintegration of the feudal system); and a second period is required when the property is sold during a rise in prices and under conditions that make industrial investment especially advantageous ... an abundant reserve supply of labour, the formation of a proletariat, an easy access to sources of raw materials, favourable conditions for the production of tools and machinery ... All sorts of contingent factors favour these conjunctions. So many encounters for the formation of the thing.

(1983: 226)

Human value, whether in the form of semi-sacred feelings of loyalty to a monarch, the warm glow of self-esteem experienced by those who consider themselves 'self-made', or the revolutionary desire to be recognized as an equal to all others, is not ultimately human in origin. Where Kant sought human value within the tight kernel of humans' own recognition of their rational powers and urged his contemporaries to find what was hidden within themselves, Deleuze and Guattari help us give an account of how human value, in its various forms, is built. For them, no kind of human value is inevitable; each kind emerges within a given organization of materials. Further, humans are not the external designers of such organizations or 'assemblages' (Deleuze and Guattari 1988: 306), but are part of their substance. Naturally, this puts limits on the degree to which we can decide upon and successfully implement a re-distribution of human value, but it certainly does not exclude the possibility of creating pockets of re-distribution, 'pores in the old social body' in which, for example, children have rights to participation in decision-making and in which their competences and those of the adults around them may change and be refreshed.

Territorialization: natural or cultural?

So far, I have suggested that some of Deleuze and Guattari's (1983, 1988) key concepts have made a non-humanist account of human value available to us. In this account, human value is built rather than discovered, and the building of value involves human activity alongside many other factors. It is vital to note that none of this implies that human value, so constructed, is false or merely imaginary. Enlightenment attempted to give substance to common human value with Kant (1983), by declaring that humans possess rational powers. This was an act of will and of determination that was focused on an ideal view of what it is to be human. Deleuze and Guattari do not primarily see human value of any kind as an ideal or as something to be willed into existence, but as an element of very real arrangements of materials.

I began my discussion of Deleuze and Guattari's (1983, 1988) work because of the potential that separability would seem to have to erode the key distinctions that give human beings special value in a world that also includes beasts and things. How, then, do Deleuze and Guattari deal with the distinction between nature and culture that is the foundation of distinctively human value? Though they give no concise answer to this question, a close examination of further illustrations of territorialization and de-territorialization should prove fruitful. The following quotation contains a good deal of Deleuze and Guattari's special jargon and some awkward translation from the original French (where the term 'steppe' is used, we might prefer 'savannah'), but it is still quite clear that, for them, the term de-territorialization applies just as well to the deep past of biological evolution as it does to the historical production of human value.

> Not only is the hand a de-territorialized ... paw; the hand thus freed is itself de-territorialized in relation to the grasping and locomotive hand of the monkey. The synergistic de-territorializations of other organs (for example, the foot) must be taken into account. So must correlative de-territorializations of the milieu: the steppe as an associated milieu more de-territorialized than the forest, exerting a selective pressure of de-territorialization upon the body and technology (it was on the steppe, not in the forest, that the hand was able appear as a free form, and fire as a technologically formable matter).
> (Deleuze and Guatarri 1988: 61)

The same sort of combinations of chance, circumstance and minor advantage that lay behind the development of dignity informed the evolutionary processes behind the development of the human hand. A paw becomes a hand adapted to grasping branches, which, as forests recede, is already de-territorialized enough to take on fresh tasks. This opens the way for the structure of the hand to change over thousands of generations into a multi-purpose organ, suited to all kinds of manipulation, from wielding a club to carving a bead. We might be inclined to insist that Deleuze and Guattari's (1983, 1988) implicit comparison between these developments masks a crucial difference between biological evolution and the cultural quality of changes in the principles underlying the distribution of human value. After all, the evolution of the hand surely involved no acts of human will, whereas cultural change does. But if we see things as Deleuze and Guattari do, this is not a false comparison. The primates and early hominids that populate their version of evolutionary history occupy a similar position to the humans who populate their version of economic and cultural history. While both will use the resources available to them to shape the world around them, neither is in control of the overall patterning of materials that they form part of and which, over time, shapes them and their lives. Territorialization and de-territorialization and the changes of form they involve are not under the complete control of primates, early hominids or humans, thus they are processes that take place outside the terms of reference of the distinction between nature and culture. Rather than thinking of human value as founded in the separation of nature from culture, of humans from beasts, Deleuze and Guattari (1983, 1988) encourage us to think of it, in its various forms, as a product of a deep and ongoing history of successive and unpredictable instances of de-territorialization and re-territorialization.

Clearly, Deleuze and Guattari owe a good deal to a tacit metaphor of evolution. Their 'evolution' is not guided by an external plan, has no determinate end and will not deliver a picture of human culture triumphing over, transcending or bursting free from nature or the material world. Human individuals are no more or less 'advanced' or 'developed' than beasts. We remain very much part of the material world. Even so, Deleuze and Guattari do not draw a simple equation between biological and cultural evolution. This is because while the formation of the hand and the formation of dignity involve processes that can be described in the same terms, they involve the alteration of matter and material relationships at different levels of analysis and over different lengths of time. Where the de-territorialization of the paw took place at the levels of bodily organs and populations, the de-territorialization of human value took place at the level of political and economic power – competition between land ownership and agricultural production, on the one hand, and trade and manufacturing, on the other. Even though different levels of activity are involved, however, it would still be inappropriate to think of these levels on the model of clearly separated 'nature' and 'culture'. This is because the processes that give rise to human value, since they take humans as part of their substance, will also inevitably involve, depend upon and potentially affect events at the level of bodily organs and populations. If there appears to be a single clear separation between nature and culture, if it makes any sense to use the two terms at all, this is as a result of the particular perspective from which we examine things. Very often it is convenient to forget just how embodied and material we are, especially when we are used to asserting our independence and separateness. Thus, Deleuze and Guattari (1983, 1988), like many of the other authors I have discussed in previous chapters, offer us a way of understanding human value that is based not on separateness but on separability.

What has this go to do with childhood?

So far I have argued that even though Deleuze and Guattari have no use for a stark separation of culture from nature, the alternative vocabulary they offer us still has the ability to recognize and to account for human value. Further, I have suggested that in their emphasis on material organization, their accounts of human value are in some ways more concrete and empirically grounded than traditional, enlightened accounts. These enlightened accounts require us first to believe that humans are essentially rational, second, to formulate a desire to realize our rational potential and, third, to achieve independence of thought and action. On Deleuze and Guattari's (1983, 1988) account, the grounds of value are arguably more 'real' since they depend far less on assertions about universal human properties and far less on the success of individual desire and will. Further, Deleuze and Guattari are sure to admit of abiding dependency.

I have followed Deleuze and Guattari's ideas through the deep past of evolutionary history and through the historical past of economic and political change. In both cases I have suggested that the effect of 'humanity', whether in the form of 'the hand' or in the form of 'dignity' is an emergent property of material assemblages such as the coupling of an environmental niche with a population of hominids or trading relations within a feudal economy. In both cases I have suggested that because human value has material substance it is constantly open to change. I now need to relate Deleuze and Guattari (1983, 1988) more explicitly to childhood, to that period of 'developmental' time that, up until recently, has been measured against a standard of separateness.

The big divisions between nature and culture and between the material and the social that have claimed the issue of human value for themselves have long led us to think of child development as a process of transcendent separation from animality and from thinghood. Thus 'the child' has been understood as someone who belongs to those intimate and minor spaces in which it is deemed safe for them to be both animal and possessed, spaces such as the mother's breast, spaces of play and make-believe, and the family home. This makes 'the child' appear to be, by nature, a stranger to those more public and consequential spaces in which the language of rights and participation is spoken. 'The child' is excluded by the apparent gulf between the minor world of intimacy and the consequential world of public life. The child also symbolizes that gulf, carrying it with her as part of her cultural identity. Thus, one of the most difficult tasks facing anyone in favour of children's rights to representation is to cross the gulf between the intimate and the public worlds. As I will argue in the following section, Deleuze and Guattari's (1983, 1988) vocabulary can help us to build a bridge to cross this gulf, to connect the intimate world of love and the public world of rights by analysing them, from the outset, in the same terms.

How do you become a person?

In Chapter 6, I drew on Winnicott's (1971) work to suggest that, among many other things, transitional phenomena allow young children to see themselves as being rather more than just a body that is possessed by and controlled by their carers. In Chapter 7, I drew on Vygotsky's (1986) work to suggest that egocentric speech is the sign that growing children are capable of taking personal possession of the common resource of spoken language in order to build the private space we call 'thought'. These sets of events are both ways of 'becoming-person'. They would seem to stand on the 'intimate' side of the great gulf of value. On the public, legal and institutional side of the gulf lies a third way of 'becoming-person', a way focussed on the idea of participation rights. In this section I will review these three 'becomings', bringing a new analysis to them that owes much to Deleuze and Guattari (1983, 1988). By the end of the section, it should be clear that the apparent gulf between the intimate and the public is less of a reality than it often seems.

In my examination of the special class of things that Winnicott (1971) calls 'transitional objects', I drew attention to their role in changing the status of babies and young children from parental possessions into persons whose self-possession can and should be respected by carers. This is a transition from the thing-like state of being a body, to the person-like state of both being and having one's body. The transitional object, as Winnicott (1971) conceives it, is the young child's first possession. It is marked as her possession by the smells and marks that constant use leave upon it. For Winnicott the transitional object is special because it is at once part of the child, by virtue of those smells and marks, and not part of the child by virtue of its independent thing-hood. When carers respect the special nature of the transitional object, by, for example, allowing a treasured piece of cloth to get dirty and smelly, they allow that the baby may be more than just her body. The transitional object, and the conflicts and compromises that surround it, provide the first footing on which the baby may enter social life as something more than a body, as someone who may, first, possess a thing and, second, possess herself.

The transitional object and the events surrounding it present a good opportunity to use Deleuze and Guattari's (1983, 1988) concepts to describe one set of intimate events in childhood. The transitional phenomenon is a relatively simple assemblage of interacting materials that includes a baby or young child, a carer and a transitional object. It is directed by no single will or design and yet it gives rise to a transformation in value – the young child's 'becoming-person'. First, the child encounters an object. It may have a soft texture that gives her sensual pleasure. Next, the carer notices this relationship between child and object and takes the opportunity it offers to encourage her to use the object as a substitute for the comfort of the carer's body. This allows the carer to minimize the child's complaints when the carer absents him or herself from the child's immediate proximity. It also converts the child's sensual pleasure into 'comfort' and strengthens the relationship between child and object. The more the object is used, the greater the comfort, since a familiar smell is added to the pleasant texture. Notice that events so far have not happened by design, but through a mutually agreeable interaction between key 'affects' (Deleuze and Guattari 1988: 260–1) of the materials involved – the child's sensuality, the softness of the object, the carers' desires both to comfort the baby and to do other things.

By the time that the carer has encouraged use of the object for comfort, the child is attached to the object, so that when the carer attempts to remove it, perhaps to wash it, the child protests the loss of comfort. All the mutually reinforcing alignments of affects so far have led to a point at which the carer must negotiate with the child about the use and location of the object. The child is now involved in possession and has thus, within the confines of this specific set of materials and interactions, been transformed into a person. Naturally, events do not always unfold in this way. Opportunities and affects may vary. For example, things will be different if nothing soft is available to the baby, or if the carer never leaves the baby's side, or, again, if the carer is indifferent to the baby's level of comfort. But the transitional object is one path through which a body is transformed into a person. In this process, materials and relationships are rearranged in such a way that, while never leaving her body, the baby or young child is de-territorialized with respect to her body. She begins to act in and react to events that unfold beyond the limits of her body, events that are distributed through space and time in ways quite unlike the bodily sensations of hunger or cold. After 'becoming-person', there is more to the baby than her body because she is sensitive to and active within events taking place outside her body. This development is just as specific a de-territorialization as the evolution of the hand or the emergence of dignity. Though it is smaller in scale and draws in less complex sets of relations, it is, like them, neither planned nor inevitable, but is just something that is likely to happen given the right conjunctions of affects. However, because of the small scale and limited range of relationships and materials involved, it is relatively easy deliberately to take part in these events so as successfully to encourage certain outcomes rather than others. It is easier to make a baby happy than it is to be a controlling force in such matters as the evolution of the hand or the distribution of value in society.

So far, I have established that the separability involved in the intimate matter of becoming-person through transitional objects can be described as a de-territorialization of the child from the body and into social life. I now turn

all parents love their children, this awareness cannot but be problematic; it demands a solution. If parents fail to or are unable to provide for or to protect their children, this should be solved by state intervention in those children's lives. Thus, the Convention contains just such provisions and these provisions are uncontroversial. It only takes one further step of awareness of how things stand for some children to realize that giving children a voice by encouraging their participation in decision-making is just as consistent with the 'natural' call of parental love as are protection and provision. Arguably, participation rights owe their place in the Convention at least in part to the awareness of parents that some parents (and other carers, institutions and states) harm and silence their children. In such cases, participation rights promise children the scope to de-territorialize from the assemblage that normally surrounds them and silences their dissent and re-territorialize onto a new assemblage in which they can become a speaking person. A pore within the parental love that is always close to possessiveness is giving grounds for the development of organizations and relationships in which children can be self-possessed.

Conclusion

Though the three forms of 'becoming-person' I have examined in this section are all composed of different materials, it is quite clear that comparable processes of de- and re-territorialization underlie them all, whether they appear to take place in intimate or in public life. Deleuze and Guattari (1983, 1988) have helped me find a connection between the small and relatively inconsequential and the larger adult world of decision-making. They make it clear that children's rights to participation need hold no special terrors for us. They are just another de-territorialization in a whole series that have shaped human existence on the level of the species and on the level of the individual. When a paw turned into a hand, it no longer 'belonged' to the ground, but that did not mean that hands stopped touching the ground. When we think in the silent privacy of our own minds, our thoughts 'belong' to us, but that does not mean they cannot be shared. When children speak their minds and seek to differ with the adults who surround them, they are taking part in a de-territorialization from their family, but this need not make them strangers.

10 Conclusion
Three themes

Introduction

This book began by pointing out that something new is happening to the way children are valued. After centuries in which they have been valued as possessions, the Convention has crystallized the idea that they may also be understood to possess themselves. In the Convention, rights to participation in decision-making accompany rights to protection and provision. I suggested that, for some, this emerging contrast between children being possessed and being self-possessed inevitably implies a conflict between love and rights. The book as a whole can be considered an attempt to demonstrate that peaceful and mutually supportive co-existence of these apparent opposites is possible. This demonstration took the form of the identification and elaboration of the concept of separability.

I also advanced the view that the peaceful co-existence of love and rights is desirable. There are three reasons for this. First, there are many circumstances in which children's status as possessions does them good and many in which it does them harm (see Chapter 1). Procedures that allow children to be separable from the adults who surround them offer opportunities to distinguish between these sets of circumstances. Second, without the idea of separability, many differences of opinion between children and adults are likely to be attended by the question of possession. Thus, parents' separation anxieties can bring a brittle emotional tone to their dealings with their own children and lead them variously to adopt an authoritarian parenting style, or a *laissez-faire* parenting style, or to fluctuate between the two. Third, being, or aspiring to be, 'modern' and 'Western' involves the desire to maximize one's value by performing separateness. As adults try to separate themselves from their bodies, from their origins and from each other so as to occupy public life more effectively, they project dependency, naturalness and embodiment onto children. These projections create a gilded cage of intimacy around children and around childhood, ensuring that, for most adults most of the time, whatever children say or do can be understood as inconsequential. A greater awareness of separability would not only alter children's cultural position, but would also offer modern Western adults an alternative to the common sense that has them assess themselves and each other through the performance of separateness.

Once I had established that modern Western societies are committed to distributing human value on the basis of separateness through an examination of Bernstein (1971) and Beck (1992), the book turned to its main purpose, the identification and elaboration of the concept of separability. To do this I chose to analyse the work of six mid-twentieth-century students of development – Gilligan (1982), Winnicott (1971), Vygotsky (1986), Elias (1994) and Deleuze and Guattari (1983, 1988). Three main themes emerged from these analyses, each of which bears on the troubled contemporary relationship between childhood and human value. By way of conclusion, I will now draw out these themes.

Separability versus separateness

As a way of understanding human value, separability poses a challenge to separateness. Separability is nothing more than the possibility of relationship, a possibility that is always involved in the generation of human value. Separateness, however, is merely a standard by which human value is distributed. In the course of Chapters 2, 3 and 4, I charted the emergence and growth of separateness as a means for distributing human value. In Chapter 2, I followed Taylor's (Taylor and Gutmann 1992) account of the fall of the honour system and the rise of the individualistic system of human value called 'dignity'. I noted that while dignity is individualistic when compared to honour, it is quite clearly based on separability rather than on separateness. The honour system valued people according to their membership of a group of nobles, measured by their proximity to the monarch. The dignity system is aware that people are members of various groups and that they have all manner of connections with each other, but it insists that when we assign them value, we must first suspend our awareness of their group membership. Dignity allows for moments of connection and affiliation and for moments of separation. Chapter 2, however, charted the emergence of another way of distributing human value that I called 'level of development'. As honour began to give way to dignity, a conservative strategy emerged in which types of human were graded on a scale that began with nature and barbarity and ended with culture and civilization. Sometimes the scale was depicted as moral. Sometimes it took on a scientific appearance. Either way, it allowed for the development and maintenance of all manner of hierarchies which all tended to place the white, male adult European at the top. The benefits of high mutual and self-regard that came with dignity were thus preserved for some and denied others, including, as representatives of the undeveloped, children.

In Chapters 3 and 4, the way that dignity remained a dream for the European majority became key to understanding the formation of major social classes in the nineteenth and early twentieth centuries and the dissolution of working-class solidarity in the late twentieth century. The place of universal dignity in the distribution of human value was taken by a class division between those middle classes who were able to perform both as connected and as separate and thus to take a full part in both informal and institutional social life, and those working classes who developed a culture that insisted on connectedness as a form of economic and psychological self-defence. By the late twentieth century, the economy and the labour market had developed so as to require ever more commitment to the performance of separateness from ever-greater segments of the workforce. This did much to dissolve working-class solidarity, thus leaving performances of separateness without coherent critique. This allowed the performance of separateness falsely to take on the appearance of the only path to dignity.

Throughout the twentieth century some of the groupings of ethnicity and gender that had been ill served by the nineteenth-century idea of level of development had found themselves in a position to challenge it. This position was granted by the toe-hold they had maintained on the labour market. The challenge took many forms, one of which was the demand to enter the labour market, a labour market that increasingly demanded performances of separateness, on the same terms as white, adult men. Children had not found themselves in a position to challenge the idea of level of development in their own case. So well into the late twentieth century, children still had to borrow their human value from the families, communities and states that possessed them. But the idea of human dignity had not disappeared. It was preserved in the legal discourse of rights, especially in the fundamentally democratic idea of rights to participation in decision-making. Even though dignity and rights are based on separability, as children's rights to participation are proposed, many modern Westerners, fixated on separateness by the requirement in working life to perform separateness and thereby to maximize their value, experience separation anxiety and resist that proposal.

This book gives a great deal of attention to separability. I first identified it in Chapter 1 in my discussion of children's rights and I elaborated on it in Chapters 5 and 6 where I discussed the novel approaches to the intimate spaces of child development that Gilligan (1982) and Winnicott (1971) took as they dealt with their predecessors' legacies. This shift of focus from public, formal, institutional discourse to intimate, private, domestic situations is designed to show that separability does not belong exclusively either to the public or to the private sphere, but is at work in each. Separability thus runs directly counter to any tendency to divide our lives into clear zones of public separateness and private connectedness. So, as an alternative to the dominance of separateness, separability challenges the divisions that still silence children and, for many adults make children's rights appear ridiculous or monstrous.

Separability, development and inclusion

If separateness is performed at all, then this performance owes everything to separability. In the case of embodiment it is clear that no actual and complete separation between social person and the body can be achieved. Yet there are processes in which the body is supplemented (Chapter 6) so that a person is formed who is capable of possessing it, or hidden (Chapter 8) to generate good standing in a community of manners. Both sets of processes hinge on separability. I have made a similar argument in the case of 'mental' separateness. The boys in Gilligan's (1982) studies appeared to know their own minds, to be self-possessed and decisive. Since they often appeared more cognitively developed than girls of the same age, we can see that the boys received some of the status benefits of performing separateness. But what circumstances allowed the boys to 'solve' moral dilemmas so rapidly and certainly? Their performance of separateness rests on a prior gendered distribution of the duty to be separate and the duty to connect, it rests, in other words, on separability. Similarly, in Chapter 7, I read Vygotsky (1986) as arguing that the individual mind, capable of private, silent thought, depends on the collectively owned and maintained institution of spoken language. The walls around our thoughts that seem to make us so fundamentally separate from one another are a product of collective action and are maintained by collective action.

If all separateness rests on separability, then everyone, adult and child, no matter how effective their performance of separateness is in gathering value to themselves, is always also attached, connected and dependent. The appearance of actual and complete separateness is an effect of the concealment of connections. Likewise, any appearance of actual and complete attachment is an effect of the concealment of separateness. I have concentrated on analysing separateness because it has the clearest links with high social status and value. For example a leader, whether a President, Prime Minister or Chief Executive Officer, will often give speeches. Isolated at the podium, their connections to and dependency on their advisers and scriptwriters are deliberately concealed. Depending on the content of the speech, this gives rise to an effect of strength of character, conviction, passion or reason, and all appear to emanate from the individual leader. This is a measure of how closely performances of separateness are associated with decision-making.

This relationship between separateness and separability does not, however, mean that adults and children do or should always occupy identical positions. As Chapters 7 and 8 demonstrate, adults and children often have quite different positions within distributions of separability. It is clear that responsibility for oneself is not, in origin, an individual property, but has been built over time, at least in part, through the development of an institution called manners. To the extent that adults or children seem to be in control of themselves, and thus able to bear responsibility, they are equally dependent on the existence and maintenance of this institution. As Elias (1994) points out, however, adults generally have a little advantage over children since they have had longer to familiarize themselves with mannerly conduct. It takes a while to become an accomplished performer of separateness. Similarly, Vygotsky (1986) tells us that possessing one's own thoughts and thinking for oneself, come after a process of development that takes time.

The value of separability as a means of examining 'thinking for oneself' and 'responsibility for oneself' is not that it makes adults and children appear equally dependent and their claims to self-possession equally bogus. It does not. Rather, it acknowledges that these two qualities are vital for decision-making processes to take place, but turns the individualist mystique that often surrounds them on its head. Children's apparent failure as individuals to be able to think and be responsible for themselves are principal reasons for their exclusion from decision-making processes. But if these qualities are, as I would argue, collective and institutional in origin, there is no reason why decision-making processes themselves should not be structured so as to assist children to be able to perform them. On this view, it is simply mistaken to reject children's rights to participation as based on a poor reflection of children's actual abilities. If the relevant articles of the Convention are to be effectively implemented, this will take the form of helping children to think for themselves and to be responsible for themselves through appropriate decision-making practices.

The twentieth-century contribution

In Chapter 2, I suggested that a good deal of contemporary scholarship that aims to change children's cultural position is based on the critique of the late nineteenth- and early twentieth-century notions of development that have defined contemporary common sense. Anti-developmental psychologists (Stainton Rogers and Stainton Rogers 1992; Burman 1994; Morss 1996) have attempted to remove 'development' from discussions of adult–child relations, by arguing that what we are supposed to be developing towards – the independent individual – is an ideological fiction. Sociologists of childhood (James and Prout 1997; James et al. 1998) have argued that our understanding of children tends, thanks to Freud (1962, 1963) and Piaget (1927, 1959), to be so universalist in form, that there is not enough recognition of the child as an independent individual.

As I argued in Chapter 2, there is much fault to be found in the highly individualistic and discriminatory ideologies of the late nineteenth and early twentieth centuries. Freud (1962, 1963) and Piaget (1927, 1959) could both have questioned their commitments to separateness and, given hindsight, I am sure that they would have done. But both Freud and Piaget made great contributions to what passes as common sense about children today. If contemporary research on childhood is oriented toward changing common sense over, say, the next 50 years, to make children's right to participation in decision-making as natural an idea as adults' rights to decision-making, it needs to follow Freud and Piaget's example. It needs to do more than criticize common sense. It needs to try to offer better sense. That is why I chose to examine the work of the generation who came after Freud and Piaget, and who worked in their shadow.

I think it is clear that mid-twentieth-century responses to developmental thought fashioned a new, more flexible and less discriminatory set of understandings of the sources of human value and differences between adults and children. I believe that the term 'separability' is one way of linking these understandings together and thus consolidating and strengthening them. All I have tried to do is to make these potentially important developments in Western self-consciousness as memorable as I can. Given the breadth and depth of the history that underlies the association between high status and separateness and given the centrality of separateness to the public, wage-earning aspects of modern, Western identities, we should not underestimate the job of work that confronts separability.

References

Alderson, P. (2000) *Young Children's Rights: Exploring Beliefs, Principles and Practice.* London: Jessica Kingsley.

Angel, R.J. and Angel, J.L. (1997) *Who Will Care for Us?: Ageing and Long-term Care in Multi-cultural America.* New York: New York University Press.

Ariès, P. (1962) *Centuries of Childhood.* London: Jonathan Cape.

Atkinson, J.J. (1903) *Primal Law.* London.

Attwood, T. (1997) *Asperger's Syndrome.* London: Taylor and Francis.

Barnett, T. and Whiteside, A. (2002) *Aids in the Twenty-first Century: Disease and Globalization.* London: Palgrave.

Beck, U. (1992) *Risk Society: Towards a New Modernity.* London: Sage.

Bernstein, B. (1971) *Class, Codes and Control,* vol. 1. London: Routledge and Kegan Paul.

Bernstein, B. (2000) *Pedagogy, Symbolic Control and Identity.* Lanham, MD: Rowman and Littlefield.

Bleuler, E. (1912) Autistic thinking, *American Journal of Psychiatry,* 69: 873–86.

Bourdieu, P. (1984) *Distinction: A Social Critique of the Judgement of Taste.* London: Routledge and Kegan Paul.

Buckingham, D. (2000) *After the Death of Childhood: Growing Up in the Age of Electronic Media.* Cambridge: Polity.

Burman, E. (1994) *Deconstructing Developmental Psychology.* London: Routledge.

Carlson, E.A. (2001) *The Unfit: The History of a Bad Idea.* New York: Cold Spring Harbor Laboratory Press.

Castells, M. (1996) *The Rise of the Network Society.* Oxford: Blackwell.

Castells, M. (1997) *The Power of Identity.* Oxford: Blackwell.

Cheesebrough, S. (2003) Young motherhood: family transmission or family transition, in G. Jones and G. Allan (eds) *Social Relations and the Life Course.* London: Palgrave Macmillan.

Chin, P. (2004) *Haiti: A Slave Revolution.* New York: International Action Centre.

Colby, A. and Kohlberg, L. (1987) *The Measurement of Moral Judgement.* Cambridge: Cambridge University Press.

Darwin, C. (1871) *The Descent of Man.* London: John Murray.

Deleuze, G. and Guattari F. (1983) *Anti-Oedipus.* Minneapolis, MN: University of Minnesota Press.

Deleuze, G. and Guattari, F. (1988) *A Thousand Plateaus.* London: Athlone.

Derrida, J. (1976) *Of Grammatology.* Baltimore, MD: Johns Hopkins University Press.

Donzelot, J. (1979) *The Policing of Families*. Baltimore, MD: Johns Hopkins University Press.

Durkheim, E. (1984) *The Division of Labour in Society*. London: Palgrave Macmillan.

Elias, N. (1994) *The Civilising Process*. Oxford: Blackwell.

Eysenck, H.J. (1985) *The Decline and Fall of the Freudian Empire*. Harmondsworth: Viking.

Foucault, M. (1971) *Madness and Civilisation: A History of Insanity in the Age of Reason*. London: Tavistock.

Freeman, M. (2002) *Human Rights: An Interdisciplinary Approach*. Cambridge: Polity.

Freud, S. (1961) *The Standard Edition of the Complete Psychological Works of Sigmund Freud*, vol. 19. London: the Hogarth Press.

Freud, S. (1962) *Totem and Taboo: Some Points of Agreement between the Mental Lives of Savages and Neurotics*. New York: W.W. Norton and Company.

Freud, S. (1963) *Civilization and its Discontents*. London: The Hogarth Press.

General Assembly of the United Nations (1989) *UN Convention on the Rights of the Child*. Available online at: www.un.org

Giddens, A. (1992) *The Transformation of Intimacy*. Cambridge: Polity Press.

Gilligan, C. (1982) *In a Different Voice: Psychological Theory and Women's Development*. Cambridge, MA: Harvard University Press.

Gilligan, C. (1988) Remapping the moral domain: new images of self in relationship, in C. Gilligan, J.V. Ward and J.M. Taylor (eds) *Mapping the Moral Domain*. Cambridge, MA: Harvard University Press.

Gilligan, C., Ward, J.V. and Taylor, J.M. (eds) (1988) *Mapping the Moral Domain*. Cambridge, MA: Harvard University Press.

Gilman, C.P. (1992) *Herland and Selected Stories by Charlotte Perkins Gilman*. New York: Signet Classics.

Giroux, H.A. (1999) *The Mouse that Roared: Disney and the End of Innocence*. London: Rowman and Littlefield.

Gomez, L. (1997) *An Introduction to Object Relations*. London: Free Association Books.

Goonsekere, S. (1998) *Children, Law and Justice: A South Asian Perspective*. New Delhi: Sage.

Gopnik, A. and Meltzoff, A.N. (1998) *Words, Thoughts and Theories*. Cambridge, MA: MIT Press.

Herrnstein, R. and Murray, C. (1994) *The Bell Curve: Intelligence and Class Structure in American Life*. New York: Free Press.

Hofstadter, D. (1999) *Gödel, Escher, Bach: An Eternal Golden Braid*. New York: Basic Books.

Hoggart, R. (1958) *The Uses of Literacy: Aspects of Working Class Life with Special Reference to Publications and Entertainments*. Harmondsworth: Penguin.

James, A., Jenks, C. and Prout, A. (1998) *Theorizing Childhood*. Oxford: Blackwell.

James, A. and Prout, A. (eds) (1997) *Constructing and Reconstructing Childhood:*

Contemporary Issues in the Sociological Study of Childhood, 2nd edn. London: Falmer.

Jones, K. (2003) *Education in Britain: 1944 to Present*. Cambridge: Polity.

Kant, I. (1983) *Perpetual Peace and Other Essays*. Indianapolis, IN: Hackett.

Klein, M. (1975a) *Love, Guilt and Reparation*. London: The Hogarth Press.

Klein, M. (1975b) *Envy, Gratitude and Other Works*. London: The Hogarth Press.

Kligman, G. (1998) *The Politics of Duplicity: Controlling Reproduction in Ceausescu's Romania*. London: University of California Press.

Kohlberg, L. (1976) Moral stages and moralization: the cognitive developmental approach, in T. Lickman (ed.) *Moral Development and Behaviour: Theory, Research and Social Issues*. New York: Holt, Rinehart and Winston.

Labov, W. (1977) *Language in the Inner City: Studies in the Black English Vernacular*. Oxford: Blackwell.

Larrain, J. (1990) *Theories of Development: Capitalism, Colonialism and Dependency*. Cambridge: Polity.

Latour, B. (1993) *We Have Never Been Modern*. Cambridge, MA: Harvard University Press.

Lee, N.M (2001) *Childhood and Society: Growing Up in an Age of Uncertainty*. Buckingham: Open University Press.

Le Guin, U.K. (2003) *The Dispossessed*. New York: Perennial Classics.

Lévi-Strauss, C. (1986) *The Raw and the Cooked*. Harmondsworth: Penguin.

Lewontin, R., Rose, S. and Kamin, L.J. (1985) *Not in our Genes*. New York: Pantheon.

Marx, K. and Engels, F. (1998) *The Communist Manifesto*. London: Penguin.

Miller, A. (1998) *Thou Shalt Not Be Aware*. New York: Farrar, Straus and Giroux.

Miller, P. (1999) *Transformations of Patriarchy in the West, 1500–1900*. Bloomington, IN: Indiana University Press.

Morss, J.R. (1996) *Growing Critical: Alternatives to Developmental Psychology*. London: Routledge.

Nevaskar, B. (1971) *Capitalists without Capitalism: The Jains of India and the Quakers of the West*. Westport, CT: Greenwood Press.

Nodding, N. (1984) *Caring: A Feminine Approach to Ethics and Moral Education*. Berkeley, CA: University of California Press.

Peel, R.A. (1997) *Marie Stopes, Eugenics and the English Birth Control Movement*. London: The Galton Institute.

Piaget, J. (1927) *The Child's Conception of the World*. London: Routledge and Kegan Paul.

Piaget, J. (1959) *The Language and Thought of the Child*. London: Routledge and Kegan Paul.

Popper, K.R. (1963) *Conjectures and Refutations: The Growth of Scientific Knowledge*. London: Routledge and Kegan Paul.

Prout, A. and Prendergast, S. (1980) 'What will I do …?' Teenage girls and the social construction of motherhood, *Sociological Review*, 28, 3: 517–36.

Purdy, L.M. (1992) *In their Best Interest? The Case against Equal Rights for Children.* Ithaca, NY: Cornell University Press.

Ruddick, S. (1989) *Maternal Thinking: Towards a Politics of Peace.* Boston, MA: Beacon Press.

Said, E. (1993) *Culture and Imperialism.* London: Chatto and Windus.

Saussure, F. de (1960) *Course in General Linguistics.* London: Owen.

Serres, M. (1991) *Le Tiers-Instruit.* Paris: François Bourin.

Shahar, S. (1992) *Childhood in the Middle Ages.* London: Routledge.

Smart, C. and Neale, B. (1999) *Family Fragments?* Cambridge: Polity.

Stainton Rogers, R. and Stainton Rogers, W. (1992) *Stories of Childhood: Shifting Agendas of Child Concern.* London: Pearson Higher Education.

Strathern, M. (1991) *Partial Connections.* Savage, MD: Rowman and Littlefield.

Taylor, C. and Gutmann, A. (1992) *Multiculturalism and the Politics of Recognition.* Princeton, NJ: Princeton University Press.

Vygotsky, L. (1986) *Thought and Language.* Boston, MA: MIT Press.

Weber, M. (2002) *The Protestant Ethic and the Spirit of Capitalism.* Oxford: Blackwell.

Winnicott, D.W. (1971) *Playing and Reality.* London: Tavistock.

Index